Stephen Byrne, A. (Antoine) Touron, Marie-Augustin Roze

Sketches of Illustrious Dominicans

St. Louis Bertrand, Julian Garces, Jerome de Loaysa

Stephen Byrne, A. (Antoine) Touron, Marie-Augustin Roze

Sketches of Illustrious Dominicans

St. Louis Bertrand, Julian Garces, Jerome de Loaysa

ISBN/EAN: 9783744659543

Printed in Europe, USA, Canada, Australia, Japan

Cover: Foto ©ninafisch / pixelio.de

More available books at **www.hansebooks.com**

SKETCHES
OF
ILLUSTRIOUS DOMINICANS:

St. Louis Bertrand, Julian Garces,
Jerome de Loaysa.

FROM THE FRENCH OF TOURON AND ROZE, OF THE ORDER OF PREACHERS.

BY

Very Rev. STEPHEN BYRNE, O.P.

Boston:
T. B. NOONAN & CO.
1884

Copyright, 1884,
By J. L. O'NEIL.

H. J. HEWITT, PRINTER, 27 ROSE STREET, NEW YORK.

Approbations.

VIDIMUS ET APPROBAVIMUS:
FR. J. R. MEAGHER, O.P.,
FR. J. L. O'NEIL, O.P.,
Revisores Deputati.

NEO-EBORACI, *die 26, Januarii,* 1884.

IMPRIMATUR:
FR. M. D. LILLY, O.P.,
Prior Provincialis Provinciæ S. Joseph.

NEO-EBORACI *die 26, Januarii,* 1884.

ST. LOUIS BERTRAND,

OF THE ORDER OF PREACHERS, APOSTLE OF NEW GRANADA.

INTRODUCTION.

THERE is a close connection among these sketches of illustrious Dominicans which leads us to publish them in one volume. They briefly record the deeds of three heroes of the Cross, whose names, among many others, add lustre to the brilliant story of the early American Church.

As such each has its interest for the student of our Catholic missionary history. But as representing the labors of the sons of St. Dominic, too often passed over in silence, they afford a particular attraction.

St. Louis Bertrand stands pre-eminent among them as the realization of the Apostle and the Saint—the only one among the missionaries of South America, save St. Francis Solano, of the Order of St. Francis, whom the Church has crowned with the glory of canonization. Wonderful as was his life, truly deserving as he is of the name of the St. Francis Xavier of the West Indies, this Apostle of New Granada is little known to American readers. Rev. Alban Butler gives his life, but Marshall, in his "Christian Missions," *does not even mention his name.* This seems a neglect hardly excusable when we remember the extent of the Saint's labors, and the fact that they have been chronicled at considerable length by the Bollandists and other writers, particularly of Spain.

We are aware that recently an elaborate life of our Saint has been published by a Dominican of the English province, Father Wilberforce. This work is written in a very pleasing style, and displays both learning and research. The present sketch is by no means intended to rival this life. Indeed, it is but just to say that our translation was made before the English work was announced, though circumstances delayed its publication. But inasmuch as this more complete life will not be accessible to many American readers, we feel that there is sufficient room for the brief sketch here presented. To those, however, who desire to learn fuller details of our Saint's life we heartily recommend Father Wilberforce's book.

We also give the lives of two other Dominicans, both foremost among the noble soldiers of Christ who carried the banner of the Cross to the savage tribes of this Western world, and who, under the purple and the mitre, never ceased to be the faithful followers of their holy Father.

As first bishop on the American continent, Julian Garces deserves special remembrance. The memory of his saintly brother, Jerome de Loaysa, should also be dear to every lover of virtue and learning. The first Bishop and Archbishop of Lima, he is the leader of the holy and illustrious line of prelates who have successively filled that great see.

As showing us types and representatives of the Dominican missionaries and the Dominican bishops of North and South America, these lives have a certain unity. They may also have a particular interest for those who read the opening chapters of our early missionary history as given in the lives of Columbus and the Venerable Las Casas, published several years ago by the translator.

The author from whose work these present sketches are chiefly taken enjoys a world-wide celebrity. Father Touron lived and wrote in the golden age of French literature. Born in 1686, he became a Dominican in early life and died in his convent in Paris in 1775. Most of his works were published before 1760. All of them are valuable, but his "Lives of the Illustrious Men of the Dominican Order" are the best known. This work received unqualified praise from Benedict XIV., doubtless the most learned pope and one of the most profound scholars of the eighteenth century. Following such a guide, we can have every confidence in the accuracy of his statements. We have used Father Roze's work in writing the sketch of Archbishop de Loaysa only.

And yet when the eye of contemplation is turned upon the broad, deep stream of English literature that keeps ever rolling on in this latter half of the nineteenth century, a feeling of misgiving is naturally excited as to the propriety of launching upon it such an antiquated-looking craft as the life of a Saint of the Catholic Church. We make the venture, however, trusting that its brevity will commend our little book to the busy people who have neither time nor inclination to read a large work, and that its historical accuracy and value will render it acceptable to others who would have no interest in its ascetic features.

The translation, it may be remarked, does not rigidly adhere to the original. We have incorporated in our text facts drawn from other sources, besides adding a number of notes which, it is hoped, will prove of interest to the reader.

CONVENT OF ST. VINCENT FERRER,
New York, January 6, 1884, *Feast of the Epiphany.*

CONTENTS.

ST. LOUIS BERTRAND, O.P., APOSTLE OF NEW GRANADA.
PAGE
Chapter I.—His Birth and Early Life, ... 1
Chapter II.—His Vocation as a Dominican, . . . 8
Chapter III.—He is ordained Priest—Death of his Father—He is appointed Master of Novices, . . 14
Chapter IV.—Commencement of his Missionary Life, . 27
Chapter V.—He asks and obtains Permission to devote himself to the American Missions—His Wonderful Success among the Natives and Spaniards, . 39
Chapter VI.—He returns to Spain—His Holy Life still continued Twelve Years, ... 67
Chapter VII.—His Last Sickness and Death—Honors paid to his Remains—His Canonization, . . . 81

JULIAN GARCES, O.P., FIRST BISHOP OF TLASCALA, NOW PUEBLA, MEXICO, ... 95

JEROME DE LOAYSA, O.P., FIRST BISHOP AND ARCHBISHOP OF LIMA, PERU.

Chapter I.—His Early Life—He is appointed Bishop of Carthagena, ... 111
Chapter II.—He is appointed First Bishop of Lima, . 120
Chapter III.—He receives the Pallium as First Archbishop of Lima—Establishment of the University, . 125
Chapter IV.—His Labors for the Advancement of Religion and the Welfare of the Natives—His Courage and Prudence, ... 132
Chapter V.—Foundation of the great Hospital of St. Anne—Death of the Archbishop, ... 144

St. Vincent Ferrer as the model of his life; for, having the honor of being his relative in the flesh, he endeavored all the more to be united to that great Saint in spirit by the imitation of his virtues.* God blessed the holy emulation of which His grace was the living principle. The most precious favor conferred upon our Saint was, that grace seems to have led him by the hand, giving him a triumph over himself, drawing him away from such occasions as might have sullied the innocence of his soul, and happily inspiring him with a contempt for earthly things, a great love of perfection in the spiritual life, and a strong desire for Heaven. This was remarked in the very infancy of our Saint; and as he grew in years he advanced in wisdom and virtue. Docile to the warnings and instructions of the interior monitor, he seems to have forestalled the teach-

---

* It is worthy of note, as recorded in the Bull of his Canonization, that St. Louis Bertrand was baptized in the same font of St. Stephen's Church, Valencia, from which St. Vincent Ferrer, almost two hundred years before, had received the saving waters of regeneration.

ing of his parents in the exercise of all the practices of a holy life. He loved retirement; he prayed much and with great fervor; and before the flesh could rebel against the spirit he had brought it to obedience by mortifications of which his tender age was scarcely capable. He was very often found on his knees in the least frequented parts of the house; and if he carefully avoided the trifles and amusements of other children, he also kept close guard against everything that might flatter his senses in regard to sleep or food. He ate very little, and when it was possible for him to elude the vigilance of his mother he slept on the bare ground or on some wretched boards.

When it became necessary for him to attend school his literary progress was remarkable. The contagion of loose example, instead of weakening his piety, only redoubled his vigilance over himself, so that the more he felt the presence of danger the more strongly did he fortify himself by the thought of the presence of God. In simplicity of heart he sought our Lord, and in his pious exercises he received the delightful assurance of divine favor. His constant occupation and joy were in pious reading, in mental prayer, in the company of devout persons whose conversation he cherished; and in the frequent reception of the holy sacraments.

A youth leading such a life could not fail to be held up as an example of goodness in the city of Valencia. Hence he was universally regarded with much respect, and went by the name of the little Saint. But his opinion of himself was very different; he hardly felt that he had made the least step towards serving God or laboring for his salvation. Whether it was to avoid human applause or to satisfy the desire of living in greater retirement, he resolved to leave home secretly, and to withdraw to a species of desert, that henceforth he might be known to God alone. He actually began to execute his purpose; and, going away, he left a most touching letter for his father, in which he gave an account of his conduct and prayed him to accede to his desire. Relying on the purity of his intention, he hoped that his parents, whose piety was remarkable, would not be displeased. In this he was mistaken. A step so little expected disconcerted the whole plan. His mother, already in feeble health, felt so keenly the absence of her best-beloved child that she was soon reduced to the last extremity. Effectual steps were soon taken to bring him back. He was hotly pursued, and overtaken when seven leagues from home. Thus had they the pleasure of placing him once more under the paternal roof.

His return filled the whole family with joy and restored the health of his mother. But from that moment no one ever supposed that he would engage in the state of marriage. He was permitted to dress as an ecclesiastic, to live in obedience to the motions of the Spirit of God, and to give vent to his feelings of charity by the distribution of alms. He was now on the right path, and his sincere piety found many ways of turning his freedom to good account and of daily acquiring new merits. Without detriment to his studies, he visited the churches and hospitals more frequently. His delight was to wait on the sick, and to console and encourage those stricken with poverty or grief. But all these works failed to satisfy his constant desire to attain the higher degrees of perfection. To imitate St. Vincent Ferrer more exactly he desired, like him, to sacrifice his liberty in the same state of life.

CHAPTER II.

HIS VOCATION AS A DOMINICAN.

AFTER many fervent prayers and much fasting, performed with the intention of knowing God's holy will, and after having practised in his father's house all the exercises of the cloister, he asked for the habit of St. Dominic in the convent of Valencia. His innocence, fervor, and reputation would at once have procured the favor which he begged with much humility and importunity, if the delicacy of his appearance and his tender age had not been against him. His father, perhaps with some exaggeration, pleaded the infirm health of his son; and, having been successful in his appeal, he built great hopes on the word of the superior of the convent of Valencia that Louis would not be received as long as he was in charge.

The boy was then only in his fifteenth

year, and, although his piety had been the admiration of all, this did not prevent him from ascribing to his sinful life the delay in his reception of the habit. He did not lose hope, however, but continued to beg the great favor of becoming a Dominican. To attain this end he used all the means that an ingenious piety could inspire, and often managed to be in the company of those whose institute he loved and whose example he longed to imitate. Sometimes he worked in their garden, that he might enjoy a little of their conversation; and he was almost constantly in their church. Not content with having spent many hours of the day in prayer, he adroitly concealed himself in the aisles of the church, so that he might pass the night also in reciting the divine office, or in hearing the exhortations of the prior to his community, and of the novice-master to his novices.

Fidelity so unflinching left no room to doubt that his vocation was from God; and this conviction soon set all other considerations aside. Father John Mico,* a man of eminent sanctity, having succeeded Father James Ferrand in the office of prior, publicly invested the holy postulant with the habit of his order, notwithstanding the representations, prayers, and even threats of his father. It was on the twenty-sixth day of August, 1544, in the nineteenth year of his age, that Louis Bertrand obtained by his perseverance what was due to his merits. His parents and all the friends of his family renewed their efforts to turn him from his purpose, insisting especially on the argument that his health was too weak to bear the rigors of the rule. The holy novice, obliged to hear all,

* Often written Micon. This remarkable man, whose renown was very great in Spain in his day, was born of humble parents in a small town of Valencia about the close of the fifteenth century. He became a Dominican priest at Salamanca, and received the doctor's cap on account of his success in studies and teaching. His reputation for preaching and holiness of life was so great that the Emperor Charles V. requested his superiors to employ him in Valencia in the work of preaching to the Moors, with a view to their conversion. This he did for several years with immense success, propagating at the same time, and with special ardor, devotion to the Holy Name.

answered wisely every reason adduced and every letter written to him in this vein ; and, as he felt that his vocation was from Heaven, he rose superior to all human difficulties, and succeeded in silencing some and in making others even approve his resolution. His father and mother were of the latter class ; they not only ceased to oppose him, but exhorted him to persevere, and felt happy in having received from Heaven a child in whom St. Vincent Ferrer seemed to live again. In effect all this was the fulfilment of the design which St. Louis Bertrand had conceived in his earliest years, and now he strove manfully to put it into execution. Thus his progress in virtue from the time in which he received the habit of St. Dominic appeared greater than ever, and fully realized the hopes of those who promoted his entrance into the order.

Among them Providence gave him as a guide one who was most competent to lead him far into the pathways of Christian and religious perfection. It was Father John

Mico, already mentioned, his first prior, and now his father-master. This was one of the few men, powerful in word and work, upon whom the Holy Spirit of God seems to delight in bestowing so many graces that nothing is wanting. The special attachment of this religious to St. Louis Bertrand, and the assistance he gave his novice in attaining a high degree of sanctity, have been a theme of praise among all admirers of the Saint himself. He governed the community of Valencia for the second time in 1544, when St. Louis Bertrand put himself under his direction. The disciple was worthy of the master. Nothing was left undone by which the seed of virtue which divine grace had planted in the soul of the youth might be brought to maturity. He learned to die to himself and to his own will, and to live only in the spirit of Jesus Christ; to love the cross, humiliation, and contempt; to attach himself to nothing that could tarnish the purity of his heart; to distinguish the gifts of nature from those of grace, and to seek no extraordinary means of advancement, but ever to cling to the humble performance of his duty as a religious.

All the lessons of virtue were deeply engraven upon his heart, and he daily added something to his stock of good works. At the completion of the year of noviceship he pronounced his solemn vows. From this time he was most assiduous in the pursuit of theological and ascetic knowledge.

CHAPTER III.

HE IS ORDAINED PRIEST—DEATH OF HIS FATHER—HE IS APPOINTED MASTER OF NOVICES.

BEFORE he had completed his twenty-second year he was ordered to prepare for ordination. It will be borne in mind that the decree of the Council of Trent, requiring twenty-four years completed as a necessary condition for ordination to the order of priesthood, had not yet been promulgated. About the close of the year 1547 he received from the Archbishop of Valencia, with the imposition of hands, the sacred dignity and power of the priesthood. From what has already been written, we may well judge what were the dispositions of soul and the renewal of faith and piety which he brought to the reception of a ministry the exercise of which requires angelic purity.

His burning love for the august Sacrament of the Altar and the merit of obedience mitigated his reluctance to have so great a dignity conferred upon him at so early an age. After his ordination he offered the divine mysteries every day, except when impeded by severe sickness. His preparation for Mass consisted of several hours' prayer; and, although habitually penitent and strictly watchful over himself, he confessed often, and with the greatest marks of sorrow. His angelic modesty, his fervor, and his tears inspired with devotion all who assisted at his Mass. It was said of him that his heart was plunged in a burning furnace and penetrated with the sacred flames of divine love, which raised him to the happy state of the Seraphim and diffused itself over his countenance.

In his whole conduct, however, a salutary fear of the divine judgment always held the first place. It was mingled with his extraordinary graces when receiving the Bread of Life. The consolations arising from his fervor in prayer were not free from it, and the rude penances which he inflicted upon himself were its necessary consequence. The sight of infinite justice, and that justice offended, often threw him into a frightful alarm, which penetrated the very marrow of his bones. That which brought joy and consolation to others often became for him a subject of sighs and sorrow. When the brethren sometimes advised him to moderate the rigor of his penances and relax his mind a little by proper recreation, he either responded with tears or replied to them in words to this effect: " Alas! you will not have me weep, and you say I must not mourn in the bitterness of my heart. Will you have me rejoice when I know that I am a miserable sinner, and cannot tell but that God has already pronounced upon me the sentence of eternal death?"

This saving fear, moderated, indeed, by equal confidence in the divine mercy, kept all his virtues in a proper balance, and ever increased in him the spirit of penance and humility. We shall not recount the different kinds of mortification to which he had recourse, and which were a continual martyrdom to his senses. He was not the first who united the most perfect innocence, guarded with jealousy from early youth, to a severe penance which lasted as long as life itself. It is the direct effect of that heavenly grace which we admire in many Christian heroes. What will astonish us, however, is that a body, naturally feeble and subject to frequent infirmities, could have so long borne the greatest austerities and almost constant vigils, besides the arduous labors of the apostolate.

To the exercise of this holy ministry he felt himself drawn by the same special attraction which first brought him to the threshold of St. Dominic's order. But he took good time to prove himself. He wished to exercise himself in obedience for several years before entering on the glorious career of the missionary. He prized too highly the advantages arising from the direction of his first guide, Father John Mico, not to desire to be with him so as to have the advantage of his counsels as long as Providence permitted. In 1548 Father Mico was appointed first superior of the convent of Lombay, founded by the Duke of Gandia,* and St. Louis begged it as a favor to accompany him thither. In the strictest concert they labored to establish in the new house the most exact observance. Ever guided by the same spirit, ever animated by the same zeal for the glory of God, they advanced with almost equal step on the road to perfection. Their example was most edifying, both to the faithful who heard their instructions and to the brethren of the order who had the happiness of a closer union with them in the house of God. Father Mico silently admired the wonderful progress of the Saint, who, on his part, carefully regarded and cheerfully followed the example of his master. His obedience after ordination was even more complete, if it were possible, than it had been during his novitiate.

But the mutual consolation arising from

* Afterwards the great St. Francis Borgia.

each other's society was of short duration. St. Louis, having heard of the sickness of his father, received from his superiors orders to make haste to Valencia to assist him on his death-bed and to console the afflicted family. He immediately set out. The tender love always entertained towards him who had been instrumental in the hands of Providence in giving him life brooked no delay. He was most assiduous in providing everything that could promote the happy death of his dear father. His firmness under these trying circumstances was also worthy of praise. He received the last sighs of his dying parent along with his blessing, and redoubled the ardor of his prayers for the repose of the departed soul.

After he had discharged this duty of filial affection obedience imposed upon him a weighty responsibility. Although not yet twenty-six years of age, he was called by the community of Valencia in September, 1551, to assume the office of novice-master. His wisdom, prudence, and charity were well known, and it was expected that the many splendid qualities which he possessed would compensate for his want of age, and give him an opportunity of being most useful in a position that is properly considered the most important in the religious life. In all this there was no mistake or disappointment. The manner in which he acquitted himself of his new charge, the prudent maxims which he followed, the number of excellent subjects he formed for the religious life, have caused him to be held up as a model for those entrusted with the care and education of novices. Like all men who know how to obey well, he also knew how to command well, and to cause his commands not only to be respected but loved. His first lesson was his own example, and he always began by realizing in himself what he desired to enforce among others. The only object of his corrections, ever guided by discretion and full of sweetness, was the spiritual advancement of his novices. His whole conduct was regulated by the great precepts of charity, and he was never suspected of acting from caprice or temper. Thus did he gain the affections of those who owed him obedience; for they never doubted that his praise or blame was for the best. They loved him, therefore, and he loved them most sincerely. Ever watchful over their spiritual and temporal wants, he sympathized with them in their weakness, moderated their ardor by well-timed penances, dissipated their fears and scruples, encouraged the timid, animated the tepid, and took equal care of the health and conversation of all. He was most careful to teach his novices how to pray and to give up their own wills. He trained them to renounce themselves and resist their special desires even in the smallest things, in order that their first victories over their own passions might dispose them to achieve in time much greater victories over the world and the devil.

Fully persuaded that he would render himself guilty before God if, in leaving faults unpunished, he permitted abuses to be introduced, and believing that it is an illusion to hope that any one not regular in his noviceship will afterwards become observant, he was extremely exact in the correction of the smallest faults. In doing this he wisely took his own time, so that he might attempt no correction except with a view to its having a good effect; and often he himself performed a part of the penance which he had imposed upon others. His earnest desire to preserve, as far as he could, the religious life in all its purity, disposed him to send back to the world without any misgivings those who, after repeated warnings and corrections, failed to make any improvement in their conduct. He was persuaded, and experience too plainly proves the truth of his judgment, that it is infinitely better and more advantageous to the whole body to have a few subjects, but of exact fidelity to their vocation, than a great number who seem willing to embrace a state of life in which holiness is professed, but who make no effort to sanctify themselves. Thus they labor, not to honor, but to dishonor the habit which they wear.

His discernment of spirits, so necessary a quality in a master of novices, was one of the most prominent traits in the character of our Saint. He gave many proofs of it. We shall mention only the following as a sample of the rest : Two young religious not yet under vows were very scrupulous. They often consulted him, and apparently manifested a great desire to regulate their consciences by his advice and to aim at the very highest perfection of their state. But they performed no part of what the novice-master required of them. He foretold that they would lay aside the religious habit. He expressed the same judgment in regard to a third novice, who wished to know what St. Louis thought of a revelation with which he considered he had been favored. " The levity of your spirit," said the Saint, " will drive you from one order to another ; you will try all, but will remain in none ; you will return to the world, where you will not be happy." His words were verified in every instance.

We cannot here give the details of the special attention given by our Saint to induce his novices to sanctify their studies, nor the practical instructions he was wont to impart to the lay brothers so as to establish them in true humility and all the other virtues pertaining to their particular calling. The good order which he introduced into his novitiate appeared to renew in the whole community the love of regular life and the spirit of fervor. His reputation became so high in the city of Valencia that many persons of all ages confidently addressed him, begging him to bring his great spiritual lights to bear upon their difficulties, doubts, and most embarrassing affairs.

And now we find Father John Mico, of whom we have already spoken, once more at the head of this community. This was the third time that the votes of his brethren had called on him to preside over this convent. So great was his deference to the sentiments of St. Louis that he was accustomed to send to him many who brought their doubts and troubles to himself. These two souls seemed to anticipate each other in mutually promoting the work of their Divine Saviour. But Louis Bertrand, no matter how highly he felt himself esteemed, looked upon himself only in the light of an humble disciple of the man who had been so long absorbed in the knowledge and practice of the law. The loss of such a friend, therefore, could not be felt less sensibly than that of his own father. Father John Mico, to whom some authors give the title of Blessed, finished his course in the convent of Valencia, August 31, 1555. Our Saint received his last words with filial affection, and witnessed with much feeling the honors paid to the memory of the deceased. Little children raised their innocent voices in proclaiming his praise, and the devotion as well as the concourse of the faithful at his funeral was extraordinary. The clergy of Valencia, both secular and regular, the viceroy and the city council, following the example of their archbishop, vied with one another in doing honor to the holy man; and a doctor, who was also a canon of the cathedral, pronounced the funeral oration from the text, "Indeed this was a just man."*

Don John de Ribera, then Archbishop of Valencia, named a commission to draw up a verbal process touching the miracles which it pleased God to work at the grave of His servant. To satisfy the devotion of the people, who in their necessities had never ceased to cry out to him as to a friend of God, it became necessary to remove his body several times. At length he was placed in the chapel dedicated to the honor of his own disciple, St. Louis Bertrand, Providence seeming to favor the union in death of the two faithful souls who had been so closely united in life; and thus they have received together the homage of the faithful.

* St. Luke xxiii. 47.

CHAPTER IV.

COMMENCEMENT OF HIS MISSIONARY LIFE.

WHEN Father Mico died St. Louis had not yet reached the middle time of life. He was then not quite thirty years old. He had, however, the consolation of seeing his novices for the most part make solid progress and furnish good grounds for the highest hopes in regard to their future career. As zeal for the salvation of souls, which had always been a special mark of his character, now became stronger than ever, he desired to combine with his other labors that of the apostolic ministry. Efforts were made to thwart him in this design. His poor health, and even his special unfitness for the function of preaching, were strongly urged. The office in which he was so successful, and in which he was doing so much to promote the best interests of his order, seemed to require his exclusive attention.

Severe attacks of sickness also were not unusual; and if he did not succumb altogether to his infirmities it was attributed to his spirit of fervor, his courage, or, more likely, to a species of miracle. His voice was neither strong nor agreeable. All of these circumstances conspired to impress upon his superiors and friends the idea that, instead of quickly spending himself on work beyond his powers, he ought rather to continue the work of forming good and holy men who would be able to bear the labors of the day and the fatigues of the apostolate. This was not the design of God in his regard, for the moment he put his hand to the work all that was thought wanting seemed to be abundantly supplied.

It was not customary to refuse anything to so holy a man, especially when he begged it with earnest perseverance. His pleadings in this case were answered by permission to preach; and his first attempt settled the question. His voice, his action, his force, all gave him the appearance of a new man.

His reputation for sanctity drew around him a multitude of hearers. He was soon called upon to preach in the largest churches, and sometimes in public places where church room was wanting. All who heard him listened carefully and were moved to a serious consideration of their spiritual affairs. The power of his words penetrated the most obdurate hearts. The most obstinate sinners retired from his preaching determined to regulate their consciences on the rules of the Gospel, and to begin a radical reform of their manners as the first step to a new life. Well would it have been for the people of Valencia if they had all turned to good account the warnings thus given them from Heaven either to avert the scourge that was hanging over their heads, or at least to profit by its visitation.

In the year 1557 a frightful plague began to afflict the kingdom of Valencia. The capital city felt the first effects of it. Commerce was interrupted, public assemblies were forbidden, and the superiors of religious houses dispersed their subjects among distant convents where the air was less infected with the seeds of contagion. Hence St. Louis Bertrand was sent in quality of vicar to the hospitium of St. Anne of Albaida. This place, being very retired, he regarded as a most suitable retreat in which he could give himself with greater liberty to the exercises of prayer and penance, waiting for the opportunity of again applying himself to the ministry of the divine word. But the contagion gradually spread itself over the whole country; and the little town of Albaida, with the neighboring hamlets, was soon included in its ravages. It furnished new material for the exercise of the charity of our Saint. He allowed no limits to be placed to his zeal, for as superior he found himself in a position to follow all its motions. The poor, the sick, the dying, and the dead, all furnished him with occasions for deeds of the most ardent devotedness. Without fear for his own safety, although he saw so many carried away by the pest, he threw himself entirely into the work of attending those stricken with its poison. He watched till death with those to whom he had given the last sacraments of the Church; others he buried, having found their bodies abandoned in the fields or on the mountains. He brought others to the hospitals when there was the least room for them; and many he conveyed to his own convent of Albaida, although the community had scarcely the means of subsistence, for he was persuaded that God would not abandon those who did such works in His honor.

The care of St. Louis for the sick, whether in their own houses or in the asylums opened for them by public charity, was often the means of bringing health to body and soul. In the decree of his canonization it is proved that he cured many by the imposition of hands and by prayer. It is related in particular that a religious named Francis Alleman, having caught the disease, was reduced to the last extremity, when he received a visit from the servant of God. Those in attendance looked only for his last moment, when St. Louis said in a confident tone that the sick man would recover. The latter took courage, began to hope against all hope, and recovered. It was thought that nothing short of a miracle could have brought about this result.

At length, through the mercy of God, the plague ceased; not so, however, the prevailing vices. The most scandalous crimes were as common as ever. Injustice, luxury, and dissipation were the every-day sins of the more wealthy, while the most dangerous ignorance prevailed among the poor, notably in the country parts. Profane swearing and blasphemy were almost as common as conversation itself; and the grossest superstitions of the ill-converted Moors had been adopted by the old Christians, who were as corrupt as the former, but less given to hiding their sins.

Among the preachers, who used tireless vigilance to instruct the people and draw them from the paths of iniquity, St. Louis Bertrand took the first rank. The fruits of his ministry were most abundant. True, indeed, the renown of his virtues gave much weight to his words ; but the greatest difficulties never repelled him when there was question of acting with force and firmness for the glory of God and the salvation of souls. Following the counsel, or rather precept, of the Gospel, he always endeavored to gain the sinner first by fraternal or secret correction. Singly and alone with each one he tried to gain his heart. He humbled himself before the guilty, and conjured them, by all the means which charity could inspire, to have pity on themselves and turn away the wrath of Heaven by works of penance. If, after these admonitions often repeated, the scandal did not cease, the Saint hesitated not to declaim publicly against public disorders. Those whose crimes were hidden, or whose hearts were less hardened, ordinarily submitted to the influence of divine grace as it fell upon them through his ministry. But it happened more than once that the most culpable, although not pointed out by name, feeling that the words of the preacher were principally addressed to them, became indignant; they determined not to be dragged out of the mire in which they wallowed, and seemed bent on defeating all his efforts in behalf of their souls.

The case is mentioned of two or three gentlemen who, blinded by their own passions or incited by the anger of their unhappy victims against our Saint, took extreme measures against him. One of them publicly insulted the minister of Jesus Christ; and, the latter being unwilling to retract a single word, the wretch attempted to throw him down from the pulpit. The attack of another is described as follows in the decree of his canonization: "A certain nobleman, thinking that St. Louis, in his denunciations of scandalous crimes, singled him out in particular, threatened him with death except the holy man would retract in public the words of his sermon. This St.

Louis refused to do, and the offended person attacked him with an arquebuse on his return from the church to the convent. But suddenly the weapon was changed into a crucifix, and the aggressor, converted by the miracle, earnestly begged pardon of God and the Saint."* This case was strictly investigated in Rome and was attested by several witnesses. The humility and modesty of St. Louis were not less remarkable. Lest his companion who witnessed the miracle should make it known before the proper time, and thereby attract public notice, which he dreaded even more than the assassin's bullet, he was forbidden to speak of it except he was questioned, which the Saint predicted would not happen for thirty years. It was not so easy to hide from public recognition the prodigious fruits of his ministry in the reconciliation of enemies and in the deliverance of the oppressed.

* On account of this event St. Louis Bertrand is represented in his pictures as bearing a crucifix whose upright beam is formed, at its lower extremity, like the stock of a gun.

He often had the consolation of reuniting in the bonds of friendship families long at variance; of putting an end to feuds, quarrels, and law-suits; of freeing from prison innocent persons who were threatened with the loss of honor, and of life itself, by the machinations and malice of powerful enemies.

Whilst he thus performed so successfully the apostolic functions he continued in charge of his novices, whose government he had been obliged to resume. The number who sought to be his disciples were so great that the Blessed Nicholas Factor, a Franciscan, was accustomed to compare him to the illustrious and Blessed Jordan of Saxony, second general of the order, who is believed to have invested one thousand persons with the habit of St. Dominic.

But he contemplated another mission. America had been discovered October 12, 1492, and the religious fervor of the most zealous priests burned for a whole century with a strong desire to convert the native inhabitants of this country. It is only natural to suppose that St. Louis Bertrand was of the number of those who wished to consume their lives on this mission. For him it was enough to arouse his zeal to know that in these vast regions there were many who were buried in the darkest idolatry and who had never heard the sweet name of Jesus Christ. He felt that he was called to instruct these savages and to shed upon them the blessed light of Gospel truth. His labors among his own brethren and among people who were of the household of the faith appeared to him as nothing compared with the glory of bringing salvation to millions of heathen souls. It was well known also that many faithful Dominicans, after having successfully worked in the conversion of the natives in some of the conquered provinces, had sealed with their blood their attachment to the faith when they sought to announce it to other tribes in countries little known.* He, too, longed

---

* Among these may be mentioned Father Louis Cancer, the martyr of Florida, who, having attempted the conversion of

for martyrdom, and daily, while celebrating the holy Mass, offered with St. Peter Martyr the fervent prayer: "Give me, O Lord! to die for Thee, as Thou hast willed to die for me." The sight of the image of the martyr St. Vincent aroused within him a burning desire to share in his sufferings, while the accounts that were then almost daily brought to Europe of the glorious triumphs and deaths of so many heroes of Christ only intensified his longing to give his life for the love of his Saviour and the salvation of souls.

the fierce inhabitants of the coast, suffered death at their hands on the 25th of June, 1549, on the shore of Espiritu Santo Bay. He is ordinarily regarded as the first martyr of Jesus Christ in the country now known as the United States. At Tampa, Hillsborough Co., Florida, in the diocese of St. Augustine, there is a church erected in his honor and known as the Church of St. Louis.

CHAPTER V.

HE ASKS AND OBTAINS PERMISSION TO DEVOTE HIM-
SELF TO THE AMERICAN MISSIONS—HIS WONDERFUL
SUCCESS AMONG THE NATIVES AND SPANIARDS.

FROM the moment of his ordination to the priesthood the thought of martyrdom was constantly before him; and the fire enkindled in his soul by charity caused him to look upon all occasions of suffering and of dying only as so many graces that it would be sinful to neglect. Hence he demanded nothing with so much ardor as to have the opportunity of shedding his blood for the sake of Him Who gave His own life for man's salvation.

A religious of his order, after having preached the Gospel several years in the West Indies, was at that time in Spain. He was preparing to return to the field of his labors, furnished with letters from his general, Father Vincent Justiniani, giving him ample powers to take with him any of the brethren willing to accompany him and likely to be useful on this arduous mission. Louis Bertrand looked upon it as a call of Providence directed to himself. With delight he offered himself to the good father. The remonstrances of his relatives, the tears of his novices, the opposition of his prior and the whole community of Dominicans in Valencia, were of no avail. He answered the friends who most opposed his design by saying that, in making his religious profession, he belonged entirely and exclusively to Jesus Christ, Whose interests alone from that moment ought to occupy his thoughts. To the assembled novices he delivered a beautiful and touching address, recommending fidelity to their vocation and the exact fulfilment of what he had taught them. Having received the benediction of his prior, which the latter could not refuse without danger of opposing the will of God, he departed from Valencia, his home and native place, on the first Sunday of Lent,

1562. Arriving next day at Xativa, a little seaport, he there found the companions of his voyage and a youth who demanded two favors of him : one was permission to follow him, and the other was to receive from his hands the habit of his order. The Saint answered that the first request could not be granted because of his extreme youth; nor the second because he was not called to the order of St. Dominic, but to that of St. Francis, which, indeed, he soon entered as a novice.

Our missionaries finally embarked at Seville, and their voyage was most successful. St. Louis, by his sweetness and modesty, soon gained the affection of the ship's officers and crew, and won the lasting respect and confidence of all by the holy example of his life. The vessel became a sort of church moving over the waters of the Atlantic, so continual was the chanting of the divine praises, and so regular were the hours of prayer during the course of each day. Whenever there were signs of danger all turned to our Saint; and one of his own brethren was the first to experience his favor with God. A pulley having fallen upon the head of this person, he was so badly injured that he lay for a time covered with blood and quite unconscious. Having recovered a little, the surgeons were preparing to dress his wound when St. Louis, after a short prayer, bathed the head of the religious with water, then applied his own head to his and cured him so perfectly that even the mark of the wound did not remain. We may well imagine the admiration of all who witnessed this fact. With one voice they gave thanks to God and expressed the conviction that the Almighty Himself was bringing this holy man to the New World to perform wonderful works.

Landing in that part of South America known as Castile d'Oro, on the west bank of the Orinoco River, in the province of Terra Firma, St. Louis hastened at once to the convent of St. Joseph, then a dependency of the province of St. John the Baptist in Peru.

His object in going to this convent was less for the sake of resting from the fatigues of the voyage than to prepare himself for missionary labors by penitential exercises. Not content with continuing the manner of life observed in Valencia, he prayed with renewed fervor, and increased his fastings and watchings in order to obtain from Heaven a blessing on the work of converting the infidels in which he was about to engage. In the course of his new career he added many austerities to his ordinary mortifications, such as lying on the bare ground, exposed not only to the unhealthy air but also to the annoyance of insects with which the country abounded. Either through disinterestedness, or love of suffering, or confidence in the care of Him Who watches over every life, or by a combination of all these motives, he refused to receive from the Spaniards or Indians the assistance usually extended to missionaries. This often caused him to feel the sharp trials of hunger, thirst, and other inconveniences of the most wretched poverty. A life so thoroughly apostolic could not fail to inspire hope in the success of its mission; and that hope was more than realized.

St. Louis was sent by his superiors to preach in different places; at one time to the Isthmus of Panama, again to the island of Tobaga; afterwards to the whole province of Carthagena and several other countries.* Everywhere he preached with much fruit, making great numbers of converts. The first grace for which our Saint prayed

* The countries here mentioned are mostly all on the northern coast of South America. The reader will bear in mind that although St. Louis Bertrand was doubtless the most prominent figure among the Dominican missionaries of South America, he was by no means among the earliest. The renowned Las Casas, so often mentioned with highest praise by English and American historians, had labored largely and most beneficially in the interests of the poor Indians fifty years before the advent of St. Louis. Thus, for instance, he was created "Protector-General" of the Indians by a decree of Cardinal Ximenes in 1517, which was confirmed by Charles V. in 1519. He devoted the whole of his long life as a priest to this object; and he was still living, an octogenarian, in the convent of Valladolid when St. Louis set out for America. We may conclude from this that the wonderful success of St. Louis may have been greatly promoted by the favorable impression made upon the natives by the previous labors of other Dominicans.

was that he might be understood by those to whom he came to announce the word of God. But this was not the only favor that signalized his apostolate. The gifts of prophecy and miracles also contributed very much to increase the multitude of souls who were the seal and the happy effect of the power he had received from God.

And this is no new thing; for we read in the holy Gospel according to St. Mark these undying words: " And these signs shall follow them that believe: In My name they shall cast out devils; they shall speak with new tongues. They shall take up serpents, and if they shall drink any deadly thing it shall not hurt them. They shall lay their hands upon the sick, and they shall recover." * History recounts the fulfilment of all these in the ministry of our apostle. By the invocation of the name of Jesus Christ he expelled evil spirits from those whom they possessed; he gave health to the sick,

---

* St. Mark xvi. 17, 18.

and inspired sentiments of faith and hope in all who heard him. He either spoke the languages of the nations to whom he announced the faith, or the nations understood him when he spoke his mother-tongue. And this latter, according to St. Thomas Aquinas, is no less a miracle. The enemies of virtue often became his enemies also; and when he tried to correct them they endeavored to remove him by poison. A mortal draught was thus once prepared for him; but though he drank it, not knowing the poison it contained, it did not harm him. All these facts, and many others which we may have occasion to mention in their proper places, are published and fully verified in the Bull of Canonization of our Saint.

We may mention here a singular event: When St. Louis was preparing to evangelize the district of Tubara, an Indian, still a heathen, who dwelt in the mountains, brought to him a child almost dead, begging him to baptize it. He had been informed that this sacrament would insure for his child an immortal and a happy life.* The Saint, admiring such sentiments in the mouth of an idolater, gave the child baptism with the name Michael. He died soon after; but the spiritual regeneration of this elected soul was the first-fruit of a large harvest in the country to which he belonged. This was so abundant and so glorious for St. Louis that in three years he brought more than ten thousand persons under the sweet yoke of Jesus Christ.† Those who were not convinced by his words nor moved by the sanctity of his life were completely subdued by the miracles which he performed in their presence. Their sick were healed by the prayer or touch of the servant of God; the evil spirits were put to flight by his mere presence; tempests

---

* This Indian had been thus taught by an Angel, as is related in the Bull of Canonization.

† These numbers may appear wonderful, but when we remember that the converts of St. Louis Bertrand were all noted for the thoroughness with which they had been instructed, and the fidelity with which they persevered in his teachings, surprise gives way to admiration, and we exclaim: Truly, here is the finger of God.

were stilled; and the most ferocious animals were tamed by the sign of the cross. The natives were more and more attracted by his instructions. They emulated one another in learning the law of the Lord; they opened their hearts to the influence of faith; they corrected their manners; they broke their idols, renounced their vain superstitions, and gladly assisted by the labor of their hands in erecting altars to the true God. A cacique,* having avowed to St. Louis that he dared not come to hear him on account of the terrible threats of the demon if he should abandon his idolatry, took courage when he saw the Saint trample under foot the very idols to which he had long offered sacrifice. He and his whole family believed in Jesus Christ; and in a short time not a single heathen was to be found in Tubara or its environs.

The faith being thus established in this country, where it is still preserved, St.

---

* An Indian chief.

Louis committed to others the care of cultivating the seed that he had planted, and resolved to bear to other places the torch of Gospel light. He visited districts known in the Indian dialects as *Cipacoa* and *Paluato*. There he met a Spanish governor, who received him with much distinction; and the natives showed no less docility in hearing the word of God than those of Tubara. Thus the labors of this apostle, who was called by the Indians *God's own religious man*, produced the most cheering results. The natives, to spare him the trouble of going to seek after them, came out of the woods and descended from the mountains to hear him. Attentive to his preaching and preparing themselves to receive baptism, they presented their little children in the meantime to secure this grace for them. One out of the many miracles recorded of him at this time was that he obtained by his prayers a copious and most necessary rain. For a long time a drought had prevailed to such an extent as to threaten the people with famine. They begged St. Louis to help them with his prayers. This was on the 24th of November. He put them off till the next day; appointed the place in which they were to assemble for prayer, and promised to meet them there, assuring them that their prayers would be heard. And so it happened. Abundant rain fell upon the earth, and the plentiful crops which followed were a symbol of the large number whom the servant of God received in that region into the household of the faith.

Some of the inhabitants of the country bordering on Paluato did not manifest such favorable dispositions. Slaves of their passions even more than of their idols, they pretended to be afraid of the wrath of their gods if they desisted from offering them sacrifices. In truth, their wickedness closed their ears against the word of God. Notwithstanding their coldness, St. Louis remained with them some time, and used all the means which his zeal could inspire to draw them from their errors. He offered to

God his prayers, his tears, and his penances, that these blind pagans might receive light from on high. But it seemed to no purpose, and he retired from them, having converted only two persons in the whole district. We shall see hereafter that God had chosen a much larger number, whom He called to the faith in His own good time.

After this apparently unsuccessful mission St. Louis, whose zeal recognized no obstacle, undertook the conversion of a people known generally as the Caribbees, in the Indian dialect *Callinagi*. They were naturally a cruel, savage, and most intractable race, and withal extremely superstitious. Hitherto the preachers of our holy faith seemed to have abandoned them to the darkness in which they appeared to be irretrievably plunged ; or, if some good priests had made the attempt to humanize and instruct them when the Spaniards first invaded Mexico, no trace of their work remained. Our Saint did not despair of their salvation. He felt that all things are possible to Him Who has marked the hours and moments in which His mercy is to be manifested. Full of this thought, and counting as nothing the sacrifice of his life, he penetrated Guiana, the country of the Caribbees, with much difficulty and hardship. He traversed forests and climbed mountains in order to find these poor infidels and persuade them to become Christians. We have no details regarding the success of this mission. Mention is made of the conversion of a cacique, and of some Negroes who had probably been taken from the Spaniards by these Indians. It appears evident that his success in this place hardly corresponded with his zeal in the cause; and we know that his perils were even greater than his fatigues. Once, having shown contempt for some special object of their idolatry, they resolved to poison him. The act followed quickly the resolution. The poison was so violent that the Saint had hardly taken it when he was attacked with terrible pains and soon reduced to the last extremity. Well satisfied to die for the glory of Jesus Christ, he offered up his life without the least regret, and embraced his crucifix more confidently and more lovingly than ever. But other labors among these infidels were in store for him. After five days of convulsive agonies he recovered, manifestly by the special providence of God, and to the great astonishment of the Indians. It was more than they could understand to see him exercising again as zealously as ever the works of his ministry, declaiming vehemently against the vanity of idols, preaching everywhere the name of Jesus Christ and the necessity of faith in Him for all who would escape the fire of hell. God Himself continued to confirm the truth of his words by new miracles. Whenever the demons assumed strange appearances or fantastic forms to impose upon their votaries or to disturb those who had embraced the faith, our Saint soon put them to flight by the sign of the cross. And although the Caribbean priests, much more stubborn in their errors than other pagans in these parts, ever resisted the ministry of St. Louis in the same manner as the magicians of Pharao had resisted Moses, he did not fail to draw great numbers to the truth. These he rescued from the darkness of idolatry as well as from the mire of iniquity.

On the mountains of St. Martha his success was very great. The people, less hardened in crime, and therefore more docile to grace, received our apostle as an angel sent from Heaven to show them the way thither. They crowded around him to hear his instructions, which they speedily reduced to practice. Their example was favorable among their neighbors. Whilst St. Louis was occupied in this mission he had the happiness of receiving fifteen hundred of the Indians of Paluato, who, as we said in another place, had at first resisted the grace of God, but who now showed every sign of true conversion. They openly declared that their journey had been undertaken for no other purpose than to receive baptism, which they had refused when it was preached to them in their own country. St. Louis adored the goodness of God ; began at once to instruct these Indians along with those of St. Martha, and before he descended from the mountain he had baptized fifteen thousand persons.

Thence he passed into the country of Mompox, and then into the island of St. Thomas, where he gained over another people to the faith of Christ and achieved new victories for the Church. The special protection of the Almighty here, as elsewhere, clearly manifested itself in his regard. One day as he was preaching under a large tree to a multitude of people, a troop of infidels, armed with arrows and rocks, were seen approaching. They were intent upon avenging their gods, as they supposed, by the death of him who threw down their idols and destroyed the groves and temples dedicated to their honor. The Saint's friends, seeing the danger, begged him to flee promptly from the fury of the barbarians. He declined the advice and exhorted his hearers to fear nothing ;

"for," said he, "they will lose all power of doing what they wish to do"; and he continued his preaching with the greatest tranquillity. What he predicted was more than realized. The infidels, having come within hearing distance of the Saint, suddenly stopped, listened in respectful silence, and two hundred of them demanded baptism, declaring themselves Christians. A cacique with his family soon followed their example, and became, in a certain sense, a preacher of the Gospel, the power and excellence of which he fully recognized.

Among the numerous conversions wrought by our Saint, the details of which are beyond our reach, the most difficult, no doubt, were those of the idolatrous priests. In truth, the rescue of these from the evil one brought upon St. Louis many persecutions. Those among the pagan priests who did not follow the example of their brethren in renouncing their superstitions became instruments of the malice of the old serpent by attacking the life and honor of the man who labored to pull down his throne. Open violence was offered to him; deadly weapons and poison were used to cause his destruction. But the protection of God foiled all these attempts upon his life. At last calumny was resorted to in order to bring discredit upon the preacher and his doctrine. To this end they employed an Indian woman who had been to all appearance lately converted, but who was unfaithful to the grace of baptism and unmindful of the instructions she had received. First she allowed herself to be corrupted by a Spaniard, and this sin brought on another. The consequence of her crime becoming manifest, and her accomplice expecting to be rigorously punished, he induced her to accuse St. Louis Bertrand. The Saint, long accustomed to the rudest trials and conscious of his innocence, continued his usual functions of prayer and preaching, whilst his enemies took pains to spread the evil report far and wide. God Himself defended him. The adulterous woman confessed her crime before the judge; and her wicked partner in guilt, forced to acknowledge the truth, would have been punished with all the severity of the law if St. Louis, by an excess of charity, had not interposed in his behalf.

Thus the man who waged unrelenting war on error and corruption was exposed not merely to the violence of barbarian infidels, but, what was much worse, to the malicious cunning of bad Christians. The slaves of evil passions left nothing undone by which to drive away this rigid censor of their libertinism or to silence him for ever. Sometimes they induced persons of bad character to visit his poor cabin at unseasonable hours, but always to their own confusion and disgrace. Again, by a more profound dissimulation, they would affect to praise him and pretend that he was unjustly treated; but whilst appearing as his panegyrists in public they secretly favored his detractors and industriously procured the spreading of evil reports against him. It is ever so in this world; when vice is reproved it seeks revenge on those who strive to check it.

But St. Louis sought only the glory of God in all things ; and as he placed all his confidence in divine aid, it was never wanting in time of need. The more his enemies sought to cry down his character the more the Almighty seemed inclined to give him greater glory by new prodigies. Often his prayers calmed the furious tempest, rendered venomous reptiles harmless, and tamed wild beasts. There were many witnesses of the accomplishment of several of his prophecies ; and so great was his influence among the people that his mere presence was sufficient to appease the most violent seditions. A remarkable instance of this took place in the island of Granada.

He was no less powerful in word and work in the city of Carthagena.* The ef-

---

* Carthagena is one of the oldest, and still continues to be one of the most important, cities of South America. It is situated on the Caribbean Sea, a few miles west of the mouth of the Magdalena River, with which it is connected by a canal.

fects of his preaching during an entire Lent were indeed extraordinary. The most obdurate sinners could not withstand the force of his eloquence, and still less the influence of his example, for a heroic firmness and a long-tried patience strongly supported the truths he delivered. Even his most signal miracles in healing the sick, and the raising to life of a dead woman by the application of his rosary, did not give greater weight to his words than his wonderful virtues.

The Indians and the Spaniards settled among them would have deemed it a great happiness to enjoy for a longer period the ministry of our apostle. For nearly eight years he had bent his whole energy to bring the former to the knowledge and faith of Christ our Lord. He labored with

---

It is only ten degrees north of the equator. It is a well-built city and a place of much trade, having a population of about ten thousand. It was founded by Pedro de Heredia in 1533, and was for a long time the principal seaport of the Spaniards in South America. It is well supplied with churches and convents.

no less zeal to moderate in the latter their tyranny and their insatiable greed for gold. The many obstacles he encountered in the latter work greatly retarded the success of his preaching, and finally determined him to return to Spain. He would not quit his mission, however, until he had endeavored to know the will of God by means of fervent prayer. He also consulted his superior, whose instructions he strictly followed. As soon as his intentions were known in America the numerous Christians of whose conversion he was the instrument united their prayers to those of the other missionary priests that he would remain with them. The religious of the convent of St. Antoninus in Carthagena used every means in their power to prevent his departure; those of the convent of Santa Fé (holy Faith) elected him prior, and their choice was confirmed by the provincial of the province of St. John the Baptist of Peru, who obliged him by a formal precept to accept the charge.

Under these circumstances the servant of God at once disposed himself to obey, and, in effect, embarked on the River Magdalena * to reach the convent of Santa Fé. But Providence seemed after all to favor his return to Spain. Violent and contrary winds prevailed to such an extent that the trip, ordinarily made in twenty-four days, was not half finished in thirty. While laboring under these difficulties shipwreck was added to their misfortunes. The boat on which our Saint and several persons were placed was capsized ; and the fortunate escape of all from a watery grave was attributed to his presence and prayers. Fifteen days after their departure a canoe was sent after the vessel, with letters for St. Louis from the general of his order, Father

---

* The Magdalena is a well-known river of South America, the general course of which is from near the equator northwardly to the Caribbean Sea. It is about nine hundred miles long and navigable for five hundred and fifty miles. The Santa Fé mentioned in the text is three hundred and fifty miles from its mouth.

Justiniani, giving him full permission to return to Spain.

Having received these letters, St. Louis sent a copy of them to his provincial, whose orders he was actually carrying out; he bade adieu to the brethren of Santa Fé * and returned to Carthagena by the same route on which he had come. In a few days he arrived at the town of Teneriffe, where a gentleman, who had no less tender regard for his person than veneration for his virtues, received him with open arms. It was soon reported that in eight days a fleet of vessels would be ready to sail from Carthagena to Spain. The good friend of our Saint prepared in haste all necessary provisions for the voyage, and when he supposed that the vessels were ready to sail he came to ask his blessing, remarking that it was time to go on board. But St. Louis answered that the time had not yet come. "I shall stay with you," said he, "for fifteen

† This is now Santa Fé de Bogota, the capital of New Granada.

days." The answer was a most agreeable surprise to the gentleman; but he did not know till after the event that the servant of God was destined to prepare his wife for a most holy death by giving her the last sacraments of the Church, and also to baptize her child prematurely born. All this happened in a few days and when the gentleman least looked for it. The horrible hissing of a serpent of immense size having frightened the poor woman, she hastily ran away and fell with fright. This caused a miscarriage and her death. The presence of our Saint could not prevent the accident; but it was of the greatest value, in the spiritual sense, both to the mother and her child.

During the three weeks' stay of St. Louis at Teneriffe he preached with his usual success; and the natives of this place showed scarcely less sorrow at his departure than was manifested in other parts of New Granada by the Indians, who were inconsolable for their loss. Down to our own times they have ever preserved the greatest veneration for the man whom God glorified in their sight, and to whose prayers, no doubt, we may attribute their perseverance in the faith which he preached. The spot in which he made his last stay with them is covered by a chapel, in which both Spaniards and Indians often assemble to pray and to obtain favors from God through the intercession of our Saint. He is commonly known by the name of the Apostle of the New World, and with reason. He is often compared with the illustrious St. Francis Xavier, who a few years previously had accomplished in Japan what St. Louis, with no less success, carried out in South America. Their preaching, their apostolic labors, and their miracles extended over a wide field the kingdom of Jesus Christ and the knowledge of His law. They subjected to His sweet yoke many barbarous tribes, and they planted the standard of the cross as the chief object of veneration among vast numbers who had before known only idols and their worship.

One of these saints finished a glorious career in seeking new nations to bring them into the true fold; whilst the other was allowed by Providence to return to his native land, there carefully to train other ministers to continue his labors in the conversion of the heathen.

CHAPTER VI.

HE RETURNS TO SPAIN—HIS HOLY LIFE STILL CONTINUED TWELVE YEARS.

WE shall not give the details, as they are found in the old authors, regarding the voyage of our Saint from Carthagena to Spain. His faith in God and his unshaken courage amid the perils of the ocean won the admiration of all on board. In the month of October, 1569, he arrived at Valencia, just seven years and six months after his departure thence for America. Nothing could exceed the demonstrations of joy with which he was received by his religious brethren and fellow-citizens. In the midst of all this joy, however, he heard of the death of his brother, also a Dominican priest, who had received the habit from his old friend, Father John Mico, and who was shipwrecked on the coast of Sardinia on his way to Lombardy. This intelligence caused our Saint to sigh more and more for the undying joys of Heaven, now possessed, as he hoped, by his younger brother.

He had not come back to Spain to lead a life of ease, and therefore he shrank from no labor with which he was charged. His wonderful tact in the instruction of novices was fully recognized, and it was once more employed in the service of religion. He was placed at the head of the community of St. Onuphrius, and afterwards of that of Valencia.* To both he was a perfect model of all virtue—a veritable, living rule. His counsels were ever found most wise and prudent; he had the familiarity of a brother, the tenderness of a father, the perfection of a saint, and the ready resources of a friend of God. Under his government the two convents became illustrious sanctuaries in which the spirit of prayer and penance was renewed with great fervor.

The love of silence and retreat, applica-

---

* He was prior of each house three years.

tion to study and labor, as well as zeal for the salvation of souls, were the prominent features of both convents. He recommended to his religious nothing so much as the good employment of time, purity of heart, and a constant endeavor to please God by being useful to their neighbor. With prudent severity he corrected anything that did not accord with the sanctity of their state; and, in order that no one could be mistaken as to the first maxim of his government, he caused to be engraven in large letters on the door of his cell these words of St. Paul: "If I yet pleased men I should not be the servant of Jesus Christ."*

A deep insight into the hearts of his religious, which was a special gift from God, greatly promoted the sanctity of some, and was for others a fresh stimulus to watch carefully over their conduct. Many examples are mentioned in which his discernment of conscience was manifest, and often

---

* Galatians i. 10.

he showed an exact knowledge of what had happened in distant lands and what would happen in the future. It is needless to add that these gifts were always used to promote God's glory, and to lead such as consulted him to greater fervor of penance and to greater constancy in the good works they had undertaken. Three or four facts, to which we shall devote only a few lines, will prove the truth of these assertions.

An ecclesiastic of high reputation in Valencia visited St. Louis one day and was coldly received. He was surprised and uneasy. But, reflecting on his manner of life, he began to understand this silent rebuke. He felt that his conduct was not what it should have been, and, having humbled himself before God in tearful penance, he was on a second visit received by the Saint with every mark of friendship and honor. On another occasion St. Louis visited, though contrary to his custom, a lady of high rank. She had hardly ever seen him except in the pulpit or at the altar. Her surprise was all the greater when he exhorted her to avert the anger of God and reform her life in certain particulars which he mentioned. The lady, being in reality a true Christian, acknowledged her fault and vowed to renounce the evil, which she had supposed was known to God alone.

Another lady, Dorothea Garcia, being extremely afflicted on account of the long absence of her husband, who was at sea, sought consolation from St. Louis. He at once told her that her husband was not dead; that she would again see him at home, and that she should pray for him, as he was in need of it. News of him soon reached Valencia. Dorothea's husband, Don Christopher Perez by name, after having been hotly pursued by the pirates of Algiers and almost shipwrecked in a tempest, came safely to port.

A certain prelate complained to the Saint regarding the vexations he suffered from a powerful nobleman living near him. Our Saint had compassion on him, but declared that the crimes of the offending party had reached their height, and that death would soon deliver his victims from further annoyance. The prophecy was literally fulfilled.

St. Teresa also received from St. Louis much consolation. She wrote to him with full confidence regarding the many difficulties and contradictions she encountered from all quarters in bringing about her great reform. He offered fervent prayers for her success, and sent her the following letter: "I have received your letter; and, since the point on which you ask my advice has reference to the honor and glory of God, I thought it best first to pray for light on the subject. This will explain the slowness of my answer. Now, I say to you in the Name of our Lord Jesus Christ: Go on as you have commenced. The Lord will assist you; and I declare in His Name that in fifty years hence your reform will be one of the most useful, one of the most renowned in the Church of God."

Our attention is again arrested by the manner in which St. Louis foretold the beginning of a religious institute even before the founder of it had conceived the idea. Here is the fact: John Augustine Adorno, a gentleman of Genoa engaged in secular pursuits, happened to come to Valencia, and visited the Dominican convent. St. Louis Bertrand had no sooner seen him than he offered all manner of friendly regards, at which all present were surprised. "Be not astonished," said the Saint; "this gentleman, who now appears to you as a worldling, will edify the Church by his sanctity, and will establish a religious order that will flourish in Italy and Spain and be of great utility in the salvation of souls." The first part of the prediction was soon verified. Adorno became strictly religious in his life and manners. The second part was also fulfilled, for he established the order of Regular Clerks, which Pope Sixtus V. confirmed under the name of Minors.*

It happened one year that, in the king-

---

* Adorno died in 1590 in the odor of sanctity.

dom of Valencia, high hopes were entertained of a rich harvest and an abundant yield of fruits of all kinds. St. Louis, on the contrary, predicted that the sins of the people would cause Providence to blast these hopes. In effect, an extraordinary drought during the early summer months killed the seeds that had been planted, and some time later excessive rains destroyed the wine-crop. This calamity and the partial failure of preceding years furnished St. Louis with many opportunities of exercising his charity towards the poor, and even of saving the lives of many. The convent of St. Onuphrius possessed very slender revenues, while that of Valencia, having a large number of religious, could hardly extend much aid to the poor. These circumstances were of no weight with the holy prior. He managed to distribute large alms every day, and strictly forbade the porter to let any one go away without assistance. In truth, so many persons were relieved openly and so many poor families were assisted privately that those who knew only a part of it declared that Providence, in reward of his faith and charity, had multiplied the money and food in his hands. His religious heartily seconded his intentions, and their charity was abundantly repaid, for God supplied all their wants.

But the principal occupation of our Saint after his return from America was the ministry of the word. In changing the scene of action he did not change his method. His labor and tears, his prayers and penances, were still the true sources of his success. With incredible zeal he fulfilled for twelve consecutive years all the functions of the apostolic life in several of the dioceses of Spain, and particularly in Valencia. Not even his special inclination for prayer and retirement, nor his infirmities of body, nor the occupations which seemed to require his constant presence in his community, could induce him to give up what he considered the essential duty of his vocation. Only God Himself, the omniscient Witness, could see the fruits of his ministry in the instruction of the ignorant, the conversion of sinners and the extirpation of vice.

Remarkable were the number and merit of the evangelical workers who were formed on the model of our Saint, and who, having received the finishing lessons from so able a master, became distinguished preachers themselves. The celebrated Jerome Baptist de Lanuza, as renowned among the preachers of the sixteenth century as he was among the bishops of the seventeenth, declared that he had received his first lessons from our Saint. He received the habit of the order in September, 1569, just one month before the return of St. Louis from America.

Following the example of the great St. Dominic, St. Louis Bertrand always brought with him on his missions a certain number of young religious who were destined for these labors. It was his delight to pray with them, to discuss with them points of dogmatic or moral theology, and even to practise outside of the convent the same exercises, day and night, as were conducted in the most regular communities. In the course of their journeys, and amid the greatest fatigues, he accustomed his companions to seek their relaxation in spiritual conversation. As he never spoke to them except about matters of edification, he gave them a high idea of religion, and strove to impress upon them that the world was only a phantom in comparison with the service of God and the glory of promoting the salvation of souls. He often repeated the maxim that humble and fervent prayer is the best means of making sermons effectual, and that words without works cannot change or even reach the heart. He often foretold the effect of missions in which he and his brethren were about to engage, and he never failed to assign to each one that part in the holy ministry to which he was specially adapted. In this way some of the fathers would bring little children together to teach them the rudiments of Christian doctrine and the best method of saying their prayers. Others were charged with the duty of giving familiar sermons to adults whose religious instruction had been neglected. He always placed himself in the audience to hear the young preachers, and he invariably encouraged beginners, so as to excite them to greater labor and progress. He was compared to the eagle, which flutters about the eaglets to teach them how to fly. In referring sometimes to the passages in the sermon that appeared to have moved the audience, he was careful to warn his disciples not to notice applause, but rather the silence, the tears, and the actions which resulted from the discourse. "If, after your sermon," he would say, "you see deadly enemies embrace each other; if ill-gotten goods are restored; if the occasions of sin are avoided; if scandals cease; if each one, in his special calling, endeavor to correct the irregularities of his conduct, then you may well say that the good seed has fallen upon good ground. But never fail to give the glory to God, without Whom you can do nothing." Such were the maxims of this apostolic man; and these he took no less care to practise himself than to impress upon those whom he desired to form in the holy ministry.

We have seen the constancy of our Saint in trials and persecutions of the most awful character when he was preaching the faith to the Indians. Now that he is universally honored and applauded on account of his miracles, prophecies, and numberless conversions, we are given occasion to admire his humility. Never was he so little in his own eyes, so sincerely humiliated before God, as when every one was calling him a saint, an apostle, another Vincent Ferrer. Never did the fear of the judgments of God which had marked his whole life so strongly impress him as when he was obliged to hear his own praises mentioned in public. If anything could have given him a distaste for the holy ministry of preaching, it would have been the approbation of men carried, as he thought, to excess. But he was too wise and too enlightened to neglect or avoid a great good through fear of an evil which he detested. He did not believe it necessary for the preservation of humility to become useless. To his last hour he labored to destroy the reign of sin ; yet he always looked upon himself as a sinner worthy only of contempt.

In these sentiments of humility and penance he accepted and bore with fortitude interior trials as well as bodily pain which made his life one long martyrdom. The sole thought of the judgments of God, and the fear of being eternally separated from Him Who is infinitely perfect and Whom he loved above all things, filled him with terror. This salutary fear took away from him all pleasure in anything that would flatter the senses or content nature. His severity with himself and his wonderful austerities would appear incredible, if we did not know the power of love in all true disciples of a crucified God.

CHAPTER VII.

HIS LAST SICKNESS AND DEATH—HONORS PAID TO
HIS REMAINS—HIS CANONIZATION.

THE tribulations which purify the just, as fire purifies gold in the crucible, became more continual and more severe during the last two years of our Saint's life. But increase of pain only served to display to greater advantage the heroic sentiments and noble firmness of his great soul. In all his trials his constant exclamation was the prayer of St. Augustine: " Here, O Lord! burn, here cut, here spare me not, that Thou mayest spare me in eternity." Not only did he persevere in his exercises of prayer and penance, but he did not wish to abstain from preaching. The people of Xativa had earnestly sought his presence amongst them to preach the Lent of 1580. Although reduced to extreme weakness and subject besides to frequent fevers and internal pains, he would not deprive them of what they so ardently desired.

Some time later he preached in the cathedral of Valencia; and we may truly say that he came down from the pulpit only to be carried to his deathbed.

The dangerous sickness into which he had fallen filled all Valencia with consternation. The Saint, on the contrary, rejoiced at the prospect and hope of being soon united to God, the only object of his loving desires. Nevertheless, though sick himself, he continued to be instrumental in restoring health to others; but some he warned of their approaching end, and advised them to prepare to meet their eternal Judge. A certain gentleman, on hearing of the Saint's sickness, came quickly to Valencia to crave his blessing and the favor of his prayers in behalf of one of his daughters, whose life was despaired of and whose death would greatly embarrass the affairs of his family. Cheerfully St. Louis spoke to him words that were prophetic:

"Your daughter will not die of this sickness; but you must admonish her to confess and receive the Holy Communion as an act of thanksgiving to God."

St. Louis Bertrand foresaw the day of deliverance from his earthly bondage. Nearly a year before the event he mentioned in confidence to some of his friends that he would die on the feast of St. Dennis, October the ninth, 1581. Among his most cherished friends were the Archbishop of Valencia and the prior of the chartreuse of *Porta Cœli*. This good man, Father Laurence de Zamora by name, hearing the prediction of our Saint, desired to verify it, and to that end committed the following words to writing: "A revelation: The friar Louis Bertrand dies on the feast of St. Dennis, 1581."* He sealed the paper upon which these words were written, and had it carefully placed in the archives of his monastery, with strict orders that it should not be opened until the

* Revelatio: Anno 1581, in festo Sancti Dionysii, moritur Frater Ludovicus Bertrandus.

feast of All Saints. However much he admired the sanctity of St. Louis and felt inclined to believe in his predictions, he still hoped that in this case they would not be fulfilled. He was confirmed in this hope when he noticed a favorable turn in the Saint's illness and that his fever seemed to cease about the month of May. The physicians having given orders that he should be moved into the country for the sake of a change of air, the Duke of Najarra and other noblemen contended with one another for the honor of entertaining him at their houses. The claim of the archbishop, Don John de Ribera, was preferred to all others, as was proper; and that distinguished prelate personally attended to the Saint with the most fraternal kindness for several months. He was most watchful to have the medicines and broths prescribed for the sick man administered at the appointed hours. He also had Mass celebrated at a convenient time, and Communion very frequently given to the Saint. Full of hope for his recovery, the archbishop often pleasantly said to St. Louis that he would falsify the prophecy. But the invariable answer was: " Remember, my lord, the day that is marked down ; I shall not live longer. I thank God for His mercy and desire only to do His will."

But all the tender care of the good prelate was unavailing, and the Saint's earnest request to be brought back to his convent could no longer be refused. The archbishop, along with the Bishop of Majorca, the son of the Duke of Gandia, and many other distinguished persons, accompanied him on his return and afterwards visited him often in his convent home. The archbishop insisted on watching with him during the night-time, and was always present when he received the holy sacraments. He carefully treasured up the Saint's words, and when he saw the end approaching he read the Gospel over him and asked in turn the blessing of St. Louis. Whilst the pious archbishop, surrounded by many of his clergy and all the religious of Valencia, was reciting the prayers for those in their agony, St. Louis Bertrand resigned his holy soul into the hands of God, his Creator, at ten o'clock in the morning of October the ninth, 1581. He was then fifty-five years and nine months old; and of these years he had spent thirty-seven in the order of St. Dominic and fifty in the penitential practices, which had commenced almost in his infancy.

The prior of the chartreuse of *Porta Cœli* did not wait for the feast of All Saints to open the paper of which we have spoken; he had it opened and read in presence of his whole community assembled for the purpose. With one voice they expressed admiration and a holy joy at the exactitude with which the prophecy was fulfilled, and gave thanks to God for this new proof of the sanctity of His servant. Heaven itself made him more illustrious by repeated miracles, by the unanimous voice of the faithful, and by the testimony of the most holy persons then living in Spain. We cannot recount in this brief sketch the number and variety of the miracles that are mentioned in the Bull of Canonization, and which were performed in Valencia in favor of those who, in their necessities, invoked the Saint's intercession. Miraculous cures were so frequent at his tomb that, to content the devotion of the people, the archbishop, one month after the death of the Saint, took the necessary steps to have him publicly venerated, with the consent of the Holy See. He appointed the Bishop of Majorca, Don Michael Spinoza, who began to take testimony in relation to this subject on the fourteenth of December, 1581. A deputation was also despatched to Pope Gregory XIII., praying His Holiness to make a formal investigation of the life and miracles of Father Louis Bertrand, with a view to his canonization. On the death of this pope, King Philip II. earnestly brought the subject to the notice of Pope Sixtus V., and apostolic commissioners were appointed to collect information in Spain and the Indies.

Many unfavorable events and the deaths of several popes retarded his canonization for some years, when the Order of St. Dominic, with renewed zeal, laid the matter before Pope Clement VIII. King Philip III., who attributed his recovery from a severe illness to the intercession of St. Louis, wrote to his minister in Rome to use all diligence in bringing the proceedings in relation to the Saint's canonization to a speedy conclusion. Clement VIII. had already canonized St. Hyacinth and St. Raymond, of the same order, and had declared St. Agnes of Montepulciano Blessed—thus showing his great esteem for the Dominican Order, to the calendar of which he now desired to add the name of St. Louis Bertrand. But, death intervening, it was left to his successors to complete the process. Pope Paul V. placed our Saint in the rank of the blessed servants of God by a decree of July twenty-ninth, 1608. At length, at the instance of Father Thomas Rocaberti, formerly general of the Order of Preachers and then Archbishop of Valencia, Pope Clement X., with much splendor and with all the solemnity usual on such occasions, performed the ceremony of canonization on the twelfth of April, 1671, nearly ninety years after the Saint's death.

All the states of his Catholic majesty the King of Spain celebrated the festival with extraordinary magnificence. The Province of New Granada especially distinguished itself.* The people of this province requested that St. Louis should be given to them as their special patron, believing that he who had drawn them to the true faith, and had so zealously instructed them in the law of the Gospel during his life, would still be their protector after his death. King Charles II. of Spain sent their request to Pope Alexander VIII., who, by a decree of the third of September, 1690, declared St.

* New Granada is now an independent state, and one of the most law-abiding and prosperous of the South American republics. The population is 2,500,000, of whom about 700,000 are civilized Indians. The capital is Santa Fé de Bogota, with a population of 60,000.

Louis Bertrand the patron and principal protector of New Granada. His Holiness required that his feast should be one of precept in that country and celebrated on the tenth of October, as the feast of St. Dennis falls on the ninth of that month.

The good odor of Christian charity which the labors and miracles of this blessed apostle have so widely diffused in the Old and the New World is in America especially cherished and held in benediction. May it please the Divine Providence to raise up in this our day in His holy Church, and particularly in the order to which St. Louis Bertrand belonged,* faithful imitators of his life and virtues—men filled with the same spirit of zeal and penance; apostles possessed of the same ardent love of God and of their neighbor; of the same invin-

---

* Pope Clement X., in a decree issued in 1671, has the following remarkable declaration: "The order of St. Dominic appears to have received, as an inheritance from Heaven, the glorious mission of bringing the great American nation to the knowledge of the true God and to the fold of the Catholic Church."

cible courage and persevering patience; of the same wonderful humility, which rendered him equally successful among Christians and the heathen; of all those virtues, in fine, which raised him to the highest degree of perfection, and finally crowned him with the honor of mankind and the glory of Heaven!

JULIAN GARCES,

OF THE ORDER OF PREACHERS, FIRST BISHOP OF TLASCALA, NOW PUEBLA, MEXICO.

Julian Garces,

*OF THE ORDER OF PREACHERS, FIRST BISHOP OF TLAS-
CALA, NOW PUEBLA, MEXICO.*

ALL students of American history are doubtless acquainted with the thrilling narrative of the expedition of Cortez from Vera Cruz to Mexico as it is given in Prescott's well-known work, "The Conquest of Mexico." His contest with the Tlascalans will be especially remembered. They were republicans in their form of government and hereditary enemies of the Mexican monarchy. They offered more stubborn opposition to the progress of the Spaniards than had been encountered in any part of the country. But once conquered and induced to enter into a treaty with the invaders, they were the most faithful allies of the latter. It is well known that one motive of the Spaniards in all these expeditions, and a very weighty one, was the conversion of the natives to the Christian faith. True, it was no easy matter to make the Indians believe in the religion of those whose lives often contradicted all the teachings of their creed. But another class of men accompanied or followed them, who united the strictest observance of evangelical morality with the most earnest zeal in making converts to our holy faith. Many of them have been eulogized in the warmest terms by all historians of every shade of religious opinion. The Dominicans, Father Olmedo, who was the companion of Cortez in his great expedition, and Las Casas, along with several Franciscans, have received unqualified praise from Mr. Prescott. This is especially noteworthy from the fact that he clearly shows himself no friend of the Catholic religion. One of the greatest yet least known of these heroic apostles of the New World was Julian Garces, at first Bishop of

Santa Maria de los Remedios de Yucatan, and afterwards first Bishop of Tlascala in Mexico. He was the first bishop on the American continent. There were bishops in the West Indies before his appointment, but none before him on the continent.*

Descended from an illustrious family of Aragon, he was born in the year 1457, and embraced the religious institute of St. Dominic in 1475. The success of his early studies did honor to his intellect as well as to his industry; and his progress in the schools of Paris was so rapid that on his return to Spain he aroused the emulation of the best scholars of his native land. The ablest amongst them confessed that in lite-

* For interesting and reliable information on the subject of the early bishoprics in America, and on the position of the Dominican missionaries, we refer the reader to two articles in the *American Catholic Quarterly Review* for January, 1879, and April, 1883, entitled respectively "The Catholic Church in the United States in the Recent Translation of Alzog," and "The American Hierarchy in its Threefold Source; Three Representative Bishops." These articles are from the pen of Dr. John Gilmary Shea, a ripe scholar, who is deeply versed in the history of the Catholic Church in America.

rary disputes he was indeed a dangerous rival. This is the testimony of Elias Antonio, of Lebrissa, himself celebrated in the universities of Spain.

Garces did not bury his talents in the ground. An excellent rhetorician, a subtle philosopher, a renowned theologian, after having taught with great applause in many cities of Aragon he preached the word of God with good effect in several provinces of Spain and at the court of Castile. Charles V. and the royal family equally admired his burning eloquence, often marked by tenderest pathos, and the apostolic liberty with which he lashed prevailing vices. His prudence and his purity of manners and mind opened to him the favor of many great personages. Among them we find Fonseca, Archbishop of Burgos, who preceded the Dominican Cardinal Loaysa as president of the Council of the Indies.

When it became known that the heroism of Hernando Cortez and the devotedness of the priests who accompanied him had secured the success of Spain and the Christian religion in Mexico, Charles V. interested himself deeply in providing bishops for that country. The Tlascalans in particular were reported as well disposed toward the Spanish crown and easily drawn into the fold of Christianity. Hence it was resolved to establish immediately among them an episcopal see, so as to give solid support to the work already so well begun. In the month of September, 1519, the very year of the conquest, his majesty presented to Pope Leo X. Father Julian Garces as a fit candidate for the new see. Owing to causes not explained, Bishop Garces was appointed to Santa Maria de los Remedios de Yucatan.

For seven years he labored in this field, but in 1526 he was transferred to Tlascala, now Puebla, in Mexico, and took possession of his new see, by an administrator, November the ninth, 1527.

He sent a number of zealous priests before him, and prepared to follow them as soon as possible.

The cause of his delay was to secure the protection of his majesty for the natives of the country, and to get time to learn their language, so that he might be understood by them and that his ministry might thereby be rendered more effective. Among his priests we find James de Loaysa, of his own order, who rendered important services among the natives, whose docility and apparent desire to be instructed in the truths of Christianity made all labors and trials light and easy in a field so inviting. These people, until then wrapped in the dark mantle of gross paganism, had adored idols or demons; yet they received the bishop with all manner of rejoicing, and their consolation was all the greater when they experienced his influence among them as a father and protector, both able and willing to defend them against the cruelty and avarice of their oppressors.

The tender charity of our prelate impelled him to make himself all to all to gain all, never counting as anything fatigue or labor, and bearing good-humoredly Indian manners so completely at variance with European customs. With the greatest kindness he taught them the catechism ; and by his familiar instructions he gave them a good knowledge of the principles of our holy faith, the requirements of Christian morals, and the maxims of the Gospel. His discourses were all the more efficacious when it was observed that he practised what he taught. His patience, humility, contempt of riches, horror of vice, zeal for religion, and desire of salvation were conspicuous in the eyes of his hearers, and moved them to inquire into his doctrine and to accept it. In truth, he was the object of their love, respect, and confidence. His constancy and invincible firmness in defending the natives from the vexatious oppression of their conquerors greatly contributed to this result and rendered his instructions doubly successful.

Although the Tlascalans had shown great fidelity and friendship to the Spaniards, and had aided them in the conquest of Mexico, they had little reason to persevere in these friendly dispositions. Their goods were often unceremoniously appropriated by their guests, and that, too, against the express will and written decree of the emperor. This was not all; for, having deprived them of their temporal possessions, they seemed inclined to rob them of eternal blessings also. In plain words, they maintained that these Indians, like all others, were unworthy of any association with the Spaniards and unfit to be received into the Christian communion. It was argued that slavery was their proper condition of life, and that they could at least be sold as prisoners taken in just war.

The contrary doctrine had been triumphantly maintained before Cardinal Ximenes and Charles V. by the great Las Casas, who was, indeed, the central figure in this grand struggle against barefaced oppression; and Bishop Garces was a faithful disciple of these generous sentiments and a tower of strength on the side of the poor natives. He regarded the sentiments of many of his own countrymen as equally contrary to humanity and injurious to religion. His noble charity was ever on the alert; and to prevent their impious views from obtaining practical effect he was resolved to risk all, even life itself. Nor was his charity of the puny or sentimental order; he carried his complaints even to the Royal Council of the Indies in Spain, and composed a work in favor of the oppressed natives, which he addressed to Pope Paul III. In the meantime, before his remonstrances could have the desired effect, he attacked the conduct of the Spaniards in their treatment of the natives, in the face of threats, violence, and false representations sent against him to Spain.

His career was indeed every way worthy of a successor of the Apostles; for he taught both Europeans and Indians that the law of Jesus Christ would subdue human passions and that His holy grace made all men equal as followers of a common Master. Our prelate, although possessing all the virtues and good qualities of a true bishop, was scantily furnished with other equipments of this important calling. In order to be able to give as much as possible to the needy and the orphan, he regulated his household affairs on the principle of strict economy. The persons composing his episcopal train were few in number and entirely of his own mind. Father James de Loaysa was the inseparable companion of his journeys and labors; a chaplain and two domestics made up the rest of his household. Thus, so far from being a burden or expense to his people, he procured them, on the contrary, every succor in time of need; and, content with the bare necessaries of life, he ever found in his revenues, although inconsiderable from the first, means of helping his people, and especially such as had been ruined by the greed of the conquerors.

Divine Providence prolonged the life of a man so useful to the Church and so indispensable for the consolation of the new Christians. He was more than seventy years of age when he sailed to America, and forty of these years he had labored without rest in the kingdoms of Aragon and Castile. But the good God gave him twenty years more to labor in the New World, and make the name and faith of Jesus Christ known and loved by a people whose origin is hardly known to this day, and whose existence had only then been discovered. To this glorious work our grand old bishop continued to devote himself till the shadows of the grave began to lower and the decrepitude of extreme age began to make itself felt. His holy life came to a close in 1547, in his ninetieth year. His body was laid in the Cathedral Church, the foundation of which he had laid, and the completion of which he had lived to see. He had also established a convent of his order in his episcopal city, which was sometimes written *Tesecalan* as well as *Tlascala.**

His last words to his Dominican brethren were "never to relinquish the work of converting the poor Indians, and never to withhold their protection from them should they be persecuted by the invaders of their country." The only legacy he left was the "Works of St. Augustine," with commentaries of his own.

Nicholas Antonio, in his "Library of Spain," gives credit to our prelate for no work except that already mentioned in favor of the Indians, which was composed in Latin and presented to the Sovereign Pontiff, Paul III., in 1536. It is quite certain that the decree issued in this year by that pope, declaring the Indians to be rational beings and fit to receive Christian teaching, was the result of this treatise, and of the reports of other holy missionaries.

* The city of Tlascala and its cathedral still exist. It had a population of 5,000 in 1870. The people are reported as intelligent and law-abiding, and mostly of Indian descent.

And now, after the lapse of three centuries and a half, the question will be raised, What has become of the work of these holy men? The answer is easy. It still remains. The Indians were Christianized, civilized, saved; and their descendants even now cherish the memory of their apostles and protectors, but for whom the whole race would have disappeared from Mexico and South America, the same as it has almost disappeared from the face of our northern continent. Out of a population of ten millions in Mexico more than one-half are totally or partially of Indian origin. The same is true of all South America. The Catholic priests, notably the Dominicans and Franciscans, saved them. Honor to whom honor is due.

JEROME DE LOAYSA,

OF THE ORDER OF PREACHERS, FIRST BISHOP AND ARCHBISHOP OF LIMA, PERU.

Jerome de Loaysa,

*OF THE ORDER OF PREACHERS, FIRST BISHOP AND ARCH-
BISHOP OF LIMA, PERU.*

CHAPTER I.

HIS EARLY LIFE—HE IS APPOINTED BISHOP OF CAR-
THAGENA.

THE life now presented to the English-speaking public displays in a peculiar manner the enlightened zeal and love of learning which characterized the principal missionaries of the Catholic Church in South America. Here we have a man who, though devoted heart and soul to the propagation of the Catholic faith among the natives of America, shows no less earnestness in furnishing them with all the appliances of the best systems of education known to Europe. Even if this good man, and others like him, were mistaken in their estimate of the capacity of the Indian to receive the scholastic training of the European, we must still admire the honest zeal which impelled him in 1549 to establish at Lima, Peru, a university endowed with all the privileges of Salamanca, in Spain.

Jerome de Loaysa, born about the close of the fifteenth century at Truxillo, in Estremadura, was the son of Don Alvarez de Carvajal and his wife, Joanna Gonzalez de Paradez. He received the habit of St. Dominic in the convent of Cordova in the year 1515. He was distinguished not only for his virtues as a novice and as a priest, but also for his literary acquirements, and, as years went on, for prudence and ability in the direction of souls. His apostolic labors finally consecrated his name in the early history of many churches of the New World.

We shall not dwell upon the applause he won as a student in the College of St. Gregory at Valladolid, or as a professor of philosophy and theology in the schools of Cordova and Granada. His humility during these years was remarkable, but it was even more conspicuous in his government of certain houses of his order, and in the absolute horror with which he was seized when he heard that he was nominated to the episcocopal dignity. He had just been honored with the doctor's cap, and was prior of the convent of Carboneras, in 1537, when the Emperor Charles V. informed him by letter that he had named him Bishop of Carthagena, in South America; and that he would not listen to any excuses, no matter how well founded they might seem to be. He therefore informed the superior of the Province of Spain that Jerome de Loaysa should accept the charge without delay, in accordance with his own earnest wish and that of the Pope. Hence the consent of the good father became a necessity.

Having, therefore, made to God the sacrifice of his repose and his life, the first care of our prelate after his consecration, which took place in 1537, and previous to his departure from Spain,* was to select among the different religious orders, especially his own, worthy ministers of the Gospel to accompany him in his arduous mission. He soon found himself surrounded by a number of excellent priests, whom he employed to the best advantage in the conversion of

* Though Father Touron makes no mention of a previous visit to America, Rev. M. A. Roze, O.P., in his work entitled "Les Dominicains in Amérique," tells us that as early as 1526 Father Loaysa, with other Dominicans, sailed from Cadiz for the Western missions. For five years he labored among the natives, when the cruelties of the Spaniards had so aroused his indignation and sympathy that, animated by the spirit which his brother-Dominicans had always displayed, he embarked for Spain to plead before Charles V. the cause of the oppressed Indians. His coming as bishop was, therefore, but a return to the scene of his former labors, though with greater powers and greater responsibilities. The emperor, more effectually to testify his interest in the success of Bishop Loaysa, generously promised to grant him anything he thought necessary or proper to ask for his new charge. In reply he promptly drew up the following requests:

1. That it would please his majesty to protect the Indians with energy and effect against their oppressors.
2. To provide means for the erection of a cathedral.
3. To erect a convent for the Dominican missionaries, and to obtain from their order six members each year for his diocese.

These requests were readily granted.

the natives, in regulating the morals of the Spaniards who were scattered over the conquered provinces, and in forming the new society upon the doctrines and maxims of the Gospel. As soon as he had distributed these missionaries through Terra Firma, and defined the location of each so that all the people living within the limits of his diocese might have spiritual assistance, he devoted himself entirely to the functions of his sacred ministry. While thus occupied with the spiritual good of his flock he did not neglect the progress of his cathedral, which was dedicated in the month of January, 1538, under the name and patronage of St. Catherine the Martyr of Alexandria.

About the same time he assembled all the priests of his diocese as a consultive body, and drew up, with their concurrence, many regulations admirably adapted to the promotion of such points of discipline as the circumstances of the country required. One of the regulations was the absolute prohibition to all ecclesiastics against carrying arms, or assuming the least sign of a military dress, or concealing in any way their own profession. As an evidence of the enlightened zeal of our Bishop, he proposed the establishment of a college at Carthagena such as was afterwards founded in Rome under the title of the Propaganda. In this college religious appointed by the Bishop were to teach the principles of our holy faith, the Latin language, philosophy, theology, and the laws and best usages of Spain to the children of the Indian chieftains and principal men. Thus he hoped to form good scholars and good subjects by spreading knowledge and loyalty through the whole country, which would thereby be better prepared to receive and practise the Christian religion.

The Bishop set about the execution of this work with his wonted energy, and there was every reason to believe that a few years would crown his exertions with success had he not been transferred to a more important post. Seeking only the glory of God and the salvation of souls through the preaching of the holy Gospel, he soon completely gained the confidence of the Indians. His kindness, his disinterestedness, his ever-active charity won for him, in a short time, the love and reverence of a people who clearly perceived that he preached to them nothing but what they saw him practise. His greatest difficulty was with those of his own nation, amongst whom the corrupt manners and unbridled avarice of many furnished constant material for the exercise of his patience. Often he was obliged to resist with firmness and courage the violence of certain officers who, in contempt of the royal ordinances to the contrary, continued to tyrannize over a people whose country and property they had invaded.

Notwithstanding the scandal thus given, which it was hard to remove and which formed a serious obstacle to the propagation of the faith, our zealous prelate successfully promoted the work of God and founded several religious institutions. The conversion of large numbers of the heathen sweetened the severe labors of his ministry, and his joy would have been full if he had found in the old Christians the same religious docility that he found in the new converts. Reprehensible as was the conduct of the former, he managed to govern all as well as circumstances permitted; and when he could not prevent the evil itself he contrived at least to prevent the scandalous effects resulting from it. His prudence and firmness were equally conspicuous. In the short period of five or six years the church of Carthagena, owing to the vigilance and zeal of its chief pastor, was well established, widely extended, and liberally endowed. A large number of Indian families who had abandoned their errors for the beautiful law of the Gospel made this city their home. The ministers of religion were constantly employed in correcting perverse habits, in destroying superstitions and evil practices, and in preparing for baptism those who sought admission into the Church. In other respects his diocese enjoyed peace, in so far as it was possible to preserve it at a time in which it was hard to set limits to the license of the conquerors.

CHAPTER II.

HE IS APPOINTED FIRST BISHOP OF LIMA.

THE death of Vincent Valverde, Bishop of Cuzco, induced Charles V. to establish another episcopal see in Peru, and this was to be at the new city of Lima, called by the Spaniards the CITY OF THE KINGS.* Pope Paul III. issued bulls for the erection of the new see in 1541, and satisfied all the wishes of the emperor by the translation of Bishop Loaysa from the See of Carthagena to that

* Lima is beautifully situated on the River Rimac, just six miles from the Pacific Ocean, and only twelve degrees south of the equator. Its foundation was laid on the sixth of January, the Feast of the Epiphany, 1535, by Francisco Pizarro, the famous conqueror of Peru. The cathedral still exists. It is a grand and massive structure, 320 feet long by 180 wide. The body of the conqueror lies beneath the main altar. The church of the Dominicans, 300 feet long by 80 wide, has the highest steeple in Lima. It measures 180 feet. Lima was called the City of the Kings because its foundation was laid on the Feast of the Epiphany, which commemorates the adoration of the kings. The name Lima is said to be a corruption of the Indian Rimac, the river on which it is built.

of Lima. Our prelate's intimate knowledge of the manners, customs, genius, and language of the Indians; his wisdom, experience, love of justice and peace; the success accorded to his labors through the goodness of Providence—all these considerations impressed both emperor and Pope with the conviction that he was the best-adapted person to spread the light of faith in this great kingdom, in the preservation of which the emperor was deeply interested. It was also justly supposed that he was more capable than any other ecclesiastic of securing obedience to the royal ordinances in favor of the Indians.

Following several other historians, Father Echard asserts that our prelate did not arrive at Lima until the twenty-second of August, 1543, six years after he had been consecrated Bishop of Carthagena. Charged with breaking and cultivating a new field, in the spiritual sense, the two races which constituted the object of his care furnished him with sufficient material upon which to exercise his zeal. The natives, buried in the darkest idolatry and in complete ignorance of Christian teaching, still continued to offer incense to idols; and their manners were as corrupt as their worship was impious. In the abundance of all things they sought only the gratification of every desire of the heart. They acknowledged no other happiness than that of the present life, and it is not surprising that they placed no restraint on their senses and brutal passions. Many of the Spaniards who had entered these rich provinces sword in hand were scarcely less debauched. It is not a calumny upon those fierce conquerors to say that most of them retained nothing of Christianity but the name.

It was necessary, therefore, to dispel the darkness of the former, to induce them to abandon the worship of the demon, and, having imparted to them the Christian faith, to regulate their morals by its teaching. It was also necessary to combat the vices of the Spaniards; to convince them that insatiable avarice was indeed idolatry, and that it was in vain for them to proclaim their adherence to the faith when their lives were a constant contradiction of their profession. Thus both had equal need of instruction, but the obstinacy of the latter was harder to overcome. Thus our good prelate found by experience that it was easier to persuade the natives of the truth of our religion than to induce his own countrymen to live according to its spirit. Obliged to work for the good of both races, he made himself all to all to gain all to Christ. No labor repelled him, for he felt that what was beyond all human energy was still possible to the power of God's holy grace. He well knew that a minister of Jesus Christ could promise himself every success if he were always true to his vocation and knew how to call to the aid of his work the means used by the Apostles in the conversion of the world—prayer, patience, and preaching. These were the identical means he always employed, and his success was proportionably great.

God prolonged his days that he might

prosecute this holy work more effectively. He gave him zealous and faithful assistants in the ministry, and by the silent operations of His Divine will removed many difficulties apparently insurmountable. The Holy See and the court of Castile, in order to mark in a special manner their confidence in our prelate, often anticipated his wishes so as to enable him to execute certain works that he considered necessary. In the space of a few years he formed an excellent body of priests, both secular and regular; laid the foundations of the grand cathedral, which still exists; established many parishes; founded convents, monasteries, colleges, and hospitals, both for the Indians and for the Spaniards, for men and for women.

CHAPTER III.

HE RECEIVES THE PALLIUM AS FIRST ARCHBISHOP OF LIMA—ESTABLISHMENT OF THE UNIVERSITY.

IN 1548 Pope Paul III. erected Lima into a metropolitan see and sent the *pallium* to Bishop Loaysa, who thus became its first archbishop, as he had been its first bishop. To give greater lustre to the *City of the Kings*, and to provide more effectually for the advancement of the new Christians, our Archbishop established a university, upon which the Pope and the Catholic king conferred the same privileges, with one slight exception, as were enjoyed by Salamanca. From the words of Father Touron, it would appear that the University of Lima takes its date actually from the year 1548. Another account gives the year of its foundation as 1571. It is likely that the latter date simply marks the occupation of the buildings intended for the institution, and that the whole system of studies had been inaugurated at the former date, 1548. Father Roze, however, gives a more minute account of this work of the Archbishop, and, though his dates vary slightly from the first mentioned, we think it well to give a considerable extract from " Les Dominicains in Amérique" :

"We have found," he says, "in other writings, that his principal instrument in the execution of this work was the Dominican Thomas de St. Martin, first Provincial of the Province of St. John the Baptist in Peru. It is a matter of so great importance that we deem it proper to relate in this place a few of the principal facts of the case. In 1550 the Provincial Father was summoned to attend a general chapter of his order to be held in Salamanca on the seventeenth of May, 1551. The citizens of Lima took occasion to confide to him several petitions to Charles V. Among them was the following: 'The citizens of

Lima, considering the extreme inconvenience and great expense of sending their sons to Madrid to be educated, humbly ask his Catholic Majesty to permit a college of general studies to be established in the convent of the Dominican Fathers in Lima, and to confer upon said college the same privileges, exemptions, and immunities as are enjoyed by the royal college of Salamanca in Spain.'

" Father Thomas executed his commission with such zeal and promptitude that before the chapter of his order was held he had already received a favorable answer from the government. Here is a literal translation of the original letter of the Queen of Spain, who, in the absence of her husband, acted as regent of the kingdom :

"'We have learned through Father Thomas of St. Martin, Provincial of the Order of Preachers in our province of Peru, that in the city of Lima there is a convent of his order well adapted to the purposes of a general college, in which the children of that country may be fully instructed in the arts and sciences; and that we are petitioned to establish in said convent such general college, with all the privileges, exemptions, and immunities enjoyed by the royal University of Salamanca;

"'We, therefore, will and ordain that in the convent named, or in some other suitable place, if the city deem it proper, a university enjoying all the privileges, exemptions, and immunities already mentioned be established as soon as possible; with this exception, however, that the University of Lima shall not have the liberty of exempting its graduates from the customary tax, as is the practice at Salamanca.

"'And we order the president and members of the royal council at Lima to obey the intentions expressed in this letter, and put them into execution with as little delay as possible.

"'Given at Valladolid, May 12, 1551.
"'JUAN DE SAMANA,
"'FOR HER MAJESTY THE QUEEN.'

"This university was opened in the convent of the Dominicans in 1553, and was carried on with great success in that place until it was transferred to the buildings which it still occupies under the name of St. Mark, in 1577, twenty-four years after it was opened." *

The immense value and practical utility of the foundations mentioned may be easily conceived. Their direct tendency was to civilize the natives and to multiply or confirm the numerous conversions constantly effected by the devoted zeal of apostolic missionaries. The aborigines, profiting by so many

* From these authorities, therefore, we can judge that the University of Lima has precedence by almost a century over that of Harvard, near Boston, which was commenced on a small scale about 1640. This is a *fact* which we commend to the *reflection* of that class who are ever ready to talk so glibly of *Romish* intolerance of science and of the fierce bigotry with which the monks or friars have always opposed the world in its pursuit of learning.

Let the reader compare this work of the Dominicans for the *natives* of South America with the operations carried on by the settlers of Massachusetts and other northern parts in their dealings with the Indians, and then let him draw his conclusions.

means of instruction provided for them, of their own accord threw down their idols, renounced their former superstition, and in large numbers submitted to the sweet yoke of the Gospel. In this age, while good men saw with sorrow the kingdom of God's holy grace proudly rejected and unity of faith torn by division, in one part of the world, they had the consolation of witnessing with what eagerness and joy these blessings were accepted in the newly-discovered countries. Two famous apostates from Catholic truth, Luther and Calvin, tore down the altars of the Christian religion in the old countries of Europe; they abolished the holy sacrifice of the Mass; they inaugurated frightful wars among the nations on account of religion; but, at the same time, innumerable souls were gathered into the Church from among the heathen nations by the devoted zeal and spirit of martyrdom displayed by Catholic priests. It is remarkable that the reformers confined their efforts and zeal for religion to their native countries, leaving to the priests of the true Church the whole glory of converting the heathen. Thus the Church wept her losses in the old world and rejoiced with a new joy over her rich harvest of souls in the new. And the Order of St. Dominic, in particular, seems to have been destined by Providence to take a prominent part in this holy work. The name of Las Casas* alone is sufficient to give glory to the order of which he was a member; and it is beyond question that his efforts to save the Indians from Spanish cruelty was the occasion, if not the cause, of so many members of his order having been entrusted with the government of the newly-established episcopal sees in Mexico and South America. It is well known that, even in his old age, he himself was appointed first Bishop of Chiapa, in Mexico.

* See his life, published in 1870 by Mr. O'Shea, New York.

CHAPTER IV.

HIS LABORS FOR THE ADVANCEMENT OF RELIGION AND THE WELFARE OF THE NATIVES—HIS COURAGE AND PRUDENCE.

ARCHBISHOP LOAYSA was the soul of the great work going on in Peru, but he was not alone in it. He gathered about him not only a large number of devoted priests of his own order, but other priests, both secular and regular, who showed the inclination and fitness necessary for success in this mission. He loved all and honored them according to their merits. Like a father among his children, he supplied the wants of all, and placed each one in the position best suited to his particular ability. He was severe, indeed, towards unworthy priests, and when he found them incorrigible he did not fail, through his influence with the Pope and the emperor, to send them back to Spain. In these circumstances, he feared neither the powerful friends of such ecclesiastics nor the enemies he might raise up against himself in the court of Spain by honestly following the dictates of his conscience. When the interests of Christ and His Church were in question his own were ignored or forgotten. The Archbishop was unremitting in his efforts for the preservation of peace in Peru; but the imprudence of certain governors and the turbulence or ambition of the first conquerors seriously impeded his efforts in this direction. Nevertheless, all acknowledged that his services were doubly useful to the Church and to the state, to the people and to the sovereign.*

An instance is at hand. When Charles V. had been fully convinced of the grievous wrongs inflicted upon the natives of Peru by their Spanish conquerors, he resolved to tolerate the evil no longer. With this view he appointed as Viceroy Don Blaise Nuñez

---

* He is highly praised for his prudence, good sense, and courage by Prescott in his history of the " Conquest of Peru," Vol. II.

Vela, a knight of Avila, a man of strict integrity but perhaps somewhat imprudent, to carry out to the letter the decrees in favor of the Indians. The military colonists of Peru became indignant; and it was reported that Nuñez himself had procured these severe ordinances against their peculiar plans in order to gratify private revenge by the ruin of some of them. Whether the suspicion was well founded or not, its evil effects were the same. Murmurs and complaints arose on all sides, and recourse was had to arms. This was in 1544. The inhabitants of Cuzco * openly opposed the execution of the ordinances. Gonzalez Pizarro, the only brother of the renowned Francisco now remaining in the province, was Procurator-General of Peru, and was deputed by his countrymen resident in and around Cuzco to wait upon the Viceroy and demand a revocation of the decrees. But he only increased the spirit of revolt; for he managed to put himself at

* The ancient Indian capital of Peru.

the head of several hundred armed men of the disaffected party, and resolved to enter Lima by force. The Viceroy, somewhat alarmed, had recourse to our Archbishop, urging him in the name of peace to use his influence with the rebels, and so prevent the evil effects of a resort to arms. The answer of Loaysa shows him to have been a man of wonderful prudence in the most trying circumstances. He agreed to confer with Pizarro and his party if Nuñez would promise to suspend the execution of the obnoxious decrees until the home government could be consulted and an answer obtained.* Nuñez accepted the condition all the more willingly for the reason that the Archbishop pledged himself to justify his (Nuñez's) conduct with the emperor.

Having secured a conveyance at Lima, the Archbishop met a part of the army near the river Apurimac. The wisdom and sweet-

* All the historians (including our own Prescott) who have written on these events agree in commending the wisdom of this plan.

ness of his words arrested for a time the designs of the principal officers. Some persons attached to the advancing army asked for his credentials before they would treat with him at all. The prelate nobly and promptly answered: "I am your chief pastor, your Archbishop. I am well known in this province; I require no credentials. Desist from further hostilities and I give you my plighted word that the new ordinances will not be executed until an answer is received from the emperor." The more moderate wished to stop at this point; but others insisted on continuing their march to Lima so as to seize the Viceroy, or, at least, to force the royal audience to send him back to Spain. The Archbishop, seeing the danger which threatened the capital, hastened back to confirm the people in the allegiance they had promised to their sovereign, and to aid the Viceroy by his counsels. Events proved that the precaution was most opportune.

But the precipitation of Nuñez threw everything into confusion. He proceeded along the coast and through the valley of Barancas. Having occupied a certain house one night, he saw on the walls the following words written in large characters : " He who will attempt to drive me out of my house will himself be driven out of the world." He concluded that this was intended for himself, and that a Spaniard named Antony Solar, a commissioner of the Department of Barancas, was the author of it. No longer able to conceal his anger, he hastened back to Lima and called Solar to him, and reproved him with having used seditious language to him and to the government. Without any formality he ordered Solar to be thrown into prison, and directed his own chaplain to prepare him for death. Solar, however, had not come alone; he was attended by trusty followers, who at once assumed a defensive attitude. In the meantime the rumor of this well-nigh fatal quarrel spread through Lima, and our Archbishop, followed by a number of the best citizens, waited upon the Viceroy, representing the irregularity of the proceeding, the evil consequences to which it might lead, and the bad effect already produced in consequence of the disturbed state of affairs. Finally, a day's respite was given to the alleged culprit, but he was not released from confinement. The royal audience, some of whom greatly disapproved of the whole conduct of the Viceroy, finally succeeded in liberating Solar.

We shall not follow the various phases of the civil wars in this unhappy country; suffice it to say that Nuñez lost his life near Quito, whither he had hastened at the head of a small army of loyalists, and Gonzalez Pizarro, his conqueror, was in turn overcome, arrested, and put to death in April, 1548, by the next royal governor, the celebrated pacificator of Peru, Pedro de la Gasca.* This governor honored our Archbi-.

* Prescott, in his second volume of the "Conquest of Peru," shows Gasca, who was a priest, to have been the ablest and best governor ever appointed for this province. It was with much skill that he secured peace and the downfall of Pizarro. And here we may remark that, of all the principal

shop in the most signal manner, and gave him the highest praise in his reports to the home government.

Peace followed the downfall of the Pizarros, and the Archbishop found time to apply himself to the special government of his diocese in spiritual matters. On the fourth of October, 1552, he convoked a provincial council, with a view to improve and elevate the morals of his flock, which had suffered detriment during the civil wars; and also to agree upon a uniform method of instructing the Indians, so that their conversion might be intelligently assured before the administration of Baptism. The council approved several short tracts prepared by the Archbishop, or by some of his brethren of the Dominican Order, as well adapted to the capacity of these people in helping them learn

conquerors, not one escaped a violent death. President Gasca held the Archbishop in the highest esteem, and made him his principal counsellor. Before his departure for Europe Gasca appointed him and two Dominican Fathers, Thomas de St. Martin and Dominic de St. Thomas, a commission to travel over the country and to fix a moderate tax for the Indians, lately enfranchised, as well as to regulate their wages.

the rudiments of Christian doctrine and the practices of our holy religion. The progress of religion was greatly favored by a comparatively long peace, interrupted only by a sedition excited by one Fernandez Giron, but which, through the Archbishop's efforts, was quickly suppressed by the dispersion of the rebel troops and the execution of their leader.* Our prelate turned this peace to good account in repairing the disorders caused by war. He visited his vast diocese, infused new vigor into the missions, multiplied parishes and religious houses, and provided liberally for the endowment of hospitals. To confirm ecclesiastical discipline not only among the clergy of his cathedral chapter, but also among all his priests, he assembled a second provincial council in Lima on the second of March, 1567.

* At the critical moment when Giron raised the standard of revolt the Viceroy, Antonio de Mendoza, had just died. The need of a supreme authority was evident to all, and by the votes of the auditors of the royal council this dignity was conferred on Archbishop Loaysa until the Catholic king could appoint a Viceroy.

He had a talent for all kinds of affairs, says Melendez; he was great in peace as well as in war. He could command an army of soldiers as well as govern his diocese. With learned men he was an accomplished scholar; with the great he knew how to be great; with the humble and poor he was the humblest of men. He was indeed " all to all to gain all to Christ."

One day the new Viceroy, Don Francisco de Toledo, speaking with our Archbishop and some of his suffragans, thought fit to use the following language: " If you, my lords, took good care of your flocks, I would not hear so much of the evils that prevail in this land, or be obliged to apply a remedy to them." The Archbishop quickly answered: " If you, my lord Viceroy, had always the zeal for God and the king which their service requires, and if you had always aided the prelates as you were bound to do, you would not now be obliged to employ such severe measures in the repression of crime. True, indeed, we bishops have need of you, as you also have need of us; for if we do not mutually assist one another, none of us can ever remedy the evils of which we hear so much."

In another circumstance he showed his firmness still more. This same Viceroy had brought with him from Spain a priest whose conduct did not come up to the standard required by our prelate. Secret and paternal admonition was, as usual, resorted to; but no good effect following from this proper course, he decided to send the clergyman back to Spain. Don Francisco de Toledo, hearing of it, repaired to the Archbishop's palace to obtain a commutation of the punishment, for it was considered disgraceful to be sent back under such circumstances. Our prelate politely refused to change the sentence, and the Viceroy, remarking that it was an insult to refuse him this favor, added threateningly that if the priest in question should be obliged to go to Spain his lordship the Archbishop ran a great risk of going along with him.

The Archbishop answered in a meek and firm tone, saying : " Your excellency may do as you please, but in this case I am inclined to think that we shall not go alone." Hearing this, the Viceroy returned to his palace without uttering a word.

CHAPTER V.

FOUNDATION OF THE GREAT HOSPITAL OF ST. ANNE
—DEATH OF THE ARCHBISHOP.

WE have now to make brief mention of some of the greatest works of Archbishop Loaysa. He erected a magnificent cathedral, which still exists, and which is probably the richest in the Western world. Besides different parishes he founded the convent of the Holy Rosary. But the work which chiefly enshrines his memory in benediction is probably the great hospital of St. Anne.

For a long time he had thought of founding a hospital for the poor Indians, who in their sickness were often left in the fields or woods, where they died without any care and frequently without the holy sacraments. This good thought worked upon him more and more as he advanced in years, and he resolved to put it into execution as soon as possible. To do so effectually he sold all that he possessed, and with the money received in return he laid the foundation of the grand hospital of St. Anne, which exists in Lima even to this day.

It was hardly ready to receive patients when he caused all the infirm Indians of Lima to be conveyed to it, and soon after had a room prepared for himself in the building, so that he might be near to help the dying and to watch over the whole establishment. The great charity and practical zeal of our holy prelate are here principally made manifest. He often took part in the humblest offices, and accompanied the physicians in their visits to the sick with a view to having their prescriptions properly carried out. But the income of his archbishopric was insufficient for the support of the hospital, and he was obliged to beg for it. He went from door to door in the city of Lima asking alms for his poor sick people, and sent letters to Spain to the same effect. The Spanish monarchs several times sent him large sums, for they had always at heart the temporal well-being of the Indians as well as their conversion.

Here is the circular letter which the Archbishop sent to his priests in regard to the hospital. It is found to-day at the head of the hospital regulations:

"Among the many things for which we shall have to render an account at the day of judgment, the first mentioned in the holy Gospel are works of piety and mercy to the poor and distressed. We are told that on the day of judgment the sovereign Judge will say to us: 'Come, ye blessed of My Father. I was hungry, and you gave me to eat; I was thirsty, and you gave me to drink; I was sick, and you cared for me; a stranger, and you took me in.'

"And, moreover, we read that the eternal Judge of men and angels will say to the wicked: 'Go, ye accursed of My Father, into everlasting fire, for when I was sick you did not care for me; when I was hungry you did not feed me; when I was thirsty you did not give me to drink.' Such is the account that the great God will require of us in the day of general judgment as to how we have conducted ourselves towards our neighbors in distress.

"Wherefore, considering the large number of poor Indians now in Lima who are sick and in want of all things, we have concluded to establish here a hospital for them, as a work most pleasing to God and most useful to the country; for, besides the care of the sick, many other works of mercy may be performed by means of this hospital.

"Indians, for instance, not yet Christian, seeing that we take care of them without the least object of self-interest and solely for the love of God, will be drawn to ask for Baptism.

"The baptized Indians will find in this hospital the care of the body, but still more the reception of the sacraments and the care of their souls.

"The Spaniards themselves, in contributing to the erection of this hospital, will find a good occasion to give alms as satisfaction for their sins, and a sure means of restoring to the Indians the property which was wrongfully taken from them, and of which many still retain unjust possession.

"Hence it is that we have resolved to establish a hospital for the Indians, and we ask now, and shall continue to ask, alms for the same until the work will have been entirely finished; and we hope that money sufficient to carry it on will never be wanting.

"Furthermore, we declare that, among the saints who are most remarkable for their devotion to the poor, St. Joachim and St. Anne, the father and mother of the Blessed Virgin, take a high rank. We desire, therefore, that our hospital be placed under the invocation and title of St. Anne."

He conferred on it an annual income of sixteen thousand crowns—a princely revenue for those days. But how did he secure such abundant means? It was admitted that the revenues of his diocese were not at all sufficient to meet the expenses necessary in providing his people with the spiritual and temporal succors of which they had need. It is explained by the fact that persons of high standing in the province, rich men and successful soldiers of fortune, put into his hands large sums of money for these good purposes. Besides, the Catholic king, Philip II., assigned to him the revenues of an entire province, trusting to his prudent management the proper employment of these funds in the support of churches, the poor, and those charged with their instruction and care.

Lima is also indebted to this distinguished man for the establishment of several houses of prayer and retreat; in particular, for the convent of the Third Order of St. Dominic, which has been the school of perfection of many Christian virgins. The illustrious St. Rose of Lima,* the good odor of whose wonderful virtues has spread itself over the Old World as well as the New, received here the first lessons of sanctity from those who had been formed to a holy life by the instructions and examples of our Archbishop.

After all these labors and toils, and after having added to the Kingdom of Jesus Christ a numerous people, the Archbishop died in the hospital of St. Anne, full of years and of merits, on the twenty-fifth of October, 1575, in the thirty-eighth year of his episcopate. Of these years he had spent six in Carthagena and thirty-two in Lima. His last wish was to be buried among the poor of this hospital.

Here we find his epitaph in the following beautiful inscription :

---

*She was born in Lima in 1586, eleven years after the death of the Archbishop, and died in the odor of sanctity in 1617, at the age of thirty-one years.

JEROME DE LOAYSA. 151

D. O. M.

CIVITATIS HUJUS ECCLESIÆ CATHEDRALIS ERECTOR,

ET PRIMUS EJUS ARCHIEPISCOPUS, CARTHAGENÆ

OLIM PRÆSUL,

ORDINIS PRÆDICATORUM ORNAMENTUM,

ILLUSTRISSIMUS DD. FR. HIERONYMUS DE LOAYSA,

CUI LIMA HANC PAROCHIAM ET XENODOCHIUM,

INDIGENÆ AMOREM ET OMNES IMITATIONEM DEBENT.

C. H. S.

RELIGIONE, CLEMENTIA, LIBERALITATE CLARUS.

OBIIT ANNO 1575, DIE 25 OCTOBRIS.

DA TUMULO FLORES; DIC ULTIMA VERBA JACENTI;

DISCE ETIAM SANCTE VIVERE; DISCE MORI.

We have added a few words to this epitaph as given by Touron. They are taken from " Les Dominicaines in Amérique," already mentioned. The author visited the scene of the holy Archbishop's labors, and copied from the monument the epitaph as given. From this work of Père Roze we also take the following: "Even to-day, in the hospital of St. Anne at Lima, in the centre of the cross formed by the four great corridors of the infirmary, there is an altar consecrated to the patroness of the hospital, and over this altar we see a painting of St. Anne, with our Archbishop kneeling at her feet. On a stone beneath the painting we find the following inscription in the Spanish language :

"'This is the portrait of Don Jerome de Loaysa, a native of Truxillo in Estremadura, of noble blood, a Dominican by profession, and a very learned man. In the year 1537 he was appointed Bishop of Carthagena; in 1541, Bishop of Lima. He finished his cathedral in September, 1543, and received the pallium as first Archbishop of Lima in 1548. He was a prelate of strict justice and extraordinary zeal. His charity was uncommonly conspicuous, especially towards the Indians, whom he tenderly loved, and for whose benefit he built this hospital in 1549. He gave it all his property in life, and his body in death. He provided for it, moreover, a yearly income of sixteen thousand crowns for the benefit of the poor, among whom he passed his life in the exercises of charity and prayer. He held two provincial councils, and governed his church (of Lima) thirty-two years, dying full of merits in 1575.'"

In closing this short sketch of the great Archbishop we may remark in justice to his memory that in all works relating to the history of Peru, and to the remarkable men it gave to America and the Church, our holy prelate is ever mentioned among the most illustrious.

www.ingramcontent.com/pod-product-compliance
Lightning Source LLC
Chambersburg PA
CBHW030246170426
43202CB00009B/647